**Level E**

W9-CAW-014

# History OF OUR Country

## PROGRAM CONSULTANTS

Sonya Abbye Taylor, Senior Associate
Professional Development Network, Inc.
(Education Consultant)
New Rochelle, N.Y.
and
Field Supervisor and Instructor
Manhattanville College
Purchase, N.Y.

Barbara C. Donahue, Principal
Burlington County Special Services School District
Westampton, N.J.

**Harcourt Achieve**

Rigby • Saxon • Steck-Vaughn

www.HarcourtAchieve.com
1.800.531.5015

# ACKNOWLEDGMENTS

**Photo Credits:** P.5 ©Bettman/CORBIS; p.6 ©Smithsonian American Art Museum, Washington, DC/Art Resource, NY; p.8 (top) ©Pawnee Women Preserving Corn, c. 1949, Albin Roy Jake, Pawnee, 1922-1960, Watercolor on paper, Museum purchase, The Philbrook Museum of Art, Tulsa, Oklahoma. 1949.17, (left) ©The Granger Collection; p.10 ©Emmanuel Faure/Superstock; p.11 (right) ©National Collection of Fine Art, Smithsonian Institution, (bottom) ©Scott Barrow, Inc./Superstock; p.12 ©The Granger Collection; p.13 (right) ©The Granger Collection, (bottom) ©Ernest Manewal/Superstock; p.14 ©George Holton/Photo Researchers; p.16 ©Bibliotheque National, France; p.23 ©Bettmann/CORBIS; p.25 © Jamestown-Yorktown Foundation; p.26 ©American Heritage Picture Collection; p.27 ©Jamestown-Yorktown Foundation; p.28 ©American Heritage Picture Collection; p.29 ©John Hancock Mutual Life Insurance Company; p.31 ©Courtesy of the Rhode Island Historical Society, RHi X3 3102. Peter Frederick Rothermel (1817-1895). The Banishment of Roger Williams, ca. 1850. Oil on canvas. 1943.3.1; p.34 ©Bettmann/CORBIS; p.35 ©The Granger Collection; p.36 ©Shelburne Museum, Shelburne, Vermont; p.37 ©The Granger Collection; p.39 ©Library Company of Philadelphia; p.41 ©The Library of Congress; p.42 ©Rhoda Sidney/PhotoEdit; p.44 ©Gary Conner/PhotoEdit; p.46 (top) ©Colonial Williamsburg Foundation, (bottom) The Granger Collection; p.47 ©The Metropolitan Museum of Art, Gift of Mrs. Russell Sage, 1909. (10.125.103) Photograph 1979 The Metropolitan Museum of Art; p.48 ©Bettmann/CORBIS; p.51 (right) ©Dictionary of American Portraits, (bottom) The Library of Congress; p.52 (top) ©Bettmann/CORBIS, (bottom) ©National Portrait Gallery/Art Resource; p.54 ©Bettmann/CORBIS; p.56 ©Courtesy of The Historical Society of Pennsylvania Collection, Atwater Kent Museum of Philadelphia; p.57 ©CORBIS; p.58 (top) ©The Granger Collection, (left) ©North Wind Picture Archives; p.60 ©State of South Carolina, Governor's Office; p.62 ©Historical Society of Pennsylvania; p.65 ©The Granger Collection; p.66 ©The Granger Collection; p.67 ©Jack Zehrt; p.68 (top) ©Bettmann/CORBIS, (bottom) ©National Portrait Gallery/Art Resource; p.69 ©Dennis Degnan/CORBIS; p.71 (both) ©National Portrait Gallery, Smithsonian Institution; p.73 ©National Gallery of Art, Smithsonian Institution; p.74 ©Leonard de Selva/CORBIS p.76 (both) ©Bettmann/CORBIS; p.78 ©Lewis and Clark at Three Forks, E.S. Paxson, Oil on Canvas, 1912, Courtesy of the Montana Historical Society; p.79 ©Bettmann/CORBIS; p.80 ©The Granger Collection; pp.81, 82 ©Bettmann/CORBIS; p.83 ©Jerome Richard Tiger, My People Awaits, 1966, tempera on paper, 1996.27.0988, Arthur & Shifra Silberman Collection, National Cowboy & Western Heritage Museum, Oklahoma City, OK; p.84 (left) ©U.S. Senate, (bottom) ©Michal Heron; p.86 ©Stanford University Museum of Art; p.87 (right) ©Abby Aldrich Rockefeller Folk Art Museum, Colonial Williamsburg Foundation, Williamsburg, VA, (bottom) ©Museum of the City of New York; p.89 ©The Library of Congress; p.90 ©Texana Collection, University of Texas; p.91 ©The Granger Collection; p.93 ©Willard Clay; p.94 ©Arizona Historical Society; pp.97, 98, 99 ©The Granger Collection; p.100 ©Yale University Art Gallery, The Mabel Brady Garvan Collection; p.101 (right) ©North Wind Picture Archives, (bottom) ©The Metropolitan Museum of Art, The Edward W.C. Arnold Collection of New York Prints, maps and Pictures, Bequest of Edward W. C. Arnold, 1954. (54.90.703) Photograph 1998 The Metropolitan Museum of Art; p.102 ©Bridgeman Art Library, London/Superstock; p.103 (right) ©Chicago Historical Society, (bottom) ©The Collection of the New-York Historical Society; p.105 (top) ©National Portrait Gallery, Smithsonian Institution, (bottom) ©Culver Pictures; p.106 ©Chicago Historical Society; p.107 ©The Granger Collection; p.109 ©Bettmann/CORBIS; p.111 (top) ©The Library of Congress, (bottom) ©Bettmann/CORBIS; p.112 (top) ©Bettmann/CORBIS, (bottom) ©The Granger Collection; p.113 (bottom) ©Chicago Historical Society; p.114 ©Bettmann/CORBIS; p.115 (top) ©National Archives, (middle right) ©The Granger Collection; p.116 (top) ©The Granger Collection, (left) ©Chicago Historical Society; p.117 ©The Library of Congress; p.118 (top) ©The Granger Collection, (left) ©Culver Pictures; p.119 ©North Wind Picture Archives; pp.122, 123 ©The Granger Collection; p.125 (top) ©American Petroleum Institute, (bottom) ©Bettmann/CORBIS; p.126 ©The Library of Congress; pp.127, 128 ©Bettmann/CORBIS; p.129 ©The Granger Collection; p.130 (both) ©International Museum of Photography at George Eastman House; p.131 (top) ©Hulton Archive/Getty Images, (right) ©International Museum of Photography at George Eastman House; p.132 (left) ©Jane Addams Memorial Collection (JAMC neg. 11), Special Collections, The University Library, University of Illinois at Chicago, (bottom) ©Museum of the City of New York; p.134 ©Nelson Gallery, Atkins Museum, Kansas City, Missouri; p.137 (left) ©National Portrait Gallery, Smithsonian Institute, (right) ©Bettmann/CORBIS; p.139 ©Solomon D. Butcher Collection/Nebraska State Historical Society; p.140 (left) ©The Library of Congress, (bottom) ©The Granger Collection; p.141 (right) ©The Granger Collection, (bottom) ©Bettmann/CORBIS; p.142 ©The Granger Collection; p.144 ©The Library of Congress; pp.146, 147 ©International Museum of Photography at George Eastman House; p.148 (left) ©The Granger Collection; p.150 (left) ©National Archives, (bottom) ©Imperial War Museum, London; p.151 (both) ©National Archives; p.152 ©Bettmann/CORBIS; p.155 (top) ©The Granger Collection; p.156 ©Fred Ward/Black Star; p.157 (left) ©Bettmann/CORBIS, (right) ©Frank Driggs Collection/Archive Photos/Getty Images; p.158 (top) ©Bettmann/CORBIS; (bottom) ©The Granger Collection; p.159 (right) ©Brown Brothers, (bottom) ©CORBIS; p.160 ©National Archives; p.161 ©UPI/Bettmann/CORBIS; p.162 ©Bettmann/CORBIS; p.163 (top) ©UPI/Bettmann/CORBIS; p.164 (left) ©M.P. & T.V. Photo Archive, (bottom) ©Culver Pictures; p.165 ©Tim Boxer; p.167 ©National Archives; p.168 (top) ©Bettmann/CORBIS, (left) ©National Archives; p.169 ©National Archives; p.170 ©Superstock; p.171 (left) ©Margaret Bourke-White/Getty Images, (right) ©Lambert/Archive Photos/Getty Images; p.172 ©The Granger Collection; p.173 (top) ©Navy Combat Art Collection, (bottom) ©The Granger Collection; p.174 (left) ©National Archives, (bottom) ©UPI/Bettmann/CORBIS; p.175 ©AP Photo/Julie Jacobson; p.177 ©Fred Mason/Photo Researchers; p.178 ©Bob Daemmrich/The Image Works; p.181 ©Bettmann/CORBIS; p.182 ©AP Photo/Bob Daugherty; p.183 (top) ©C.L. Chyslin, (bottom) ©AFP/Bettmann/CORBIS; p.184 ©UPI/Bettmann/CORBIS; p.185 ©George W. Bush Campaign Headquarters; pp.186, 188 ©Superstock; p.189 (top) ©Lyndon Baines Johnson Library, (bottom) ©Francis Kelley/Time Life Magazine/Getty Images; p.190 (top) ©Arthur Grace/CORBIS, (bottom) ©Robert Schoenbaum/Black Star; p.191 (right) ©Superstock, (bottom) ©NASA; p.192 (left) ©Larry Mulvehill/Photo Researchers, (bottom) ©UPI/Bettmann/CORBIS; p.193 (right) ©Jim Corwin/Photo Researchers, (bottom) ©Nicholas DeSciose/Photo Researchers; p.194 (left) ©A. Tannenbaum/CORBIS, (bottom) ©Larry Kolvoord/The Image Works; p.195 ©Bettmann/CORBIS; p.196 ©Superstock; p.199 ©Fred Ward/Black Star.

Additional photography by Comstock Royalty Free, Getty Images Royalty Free, Photos.com Royalty Free, and Royalty-Free/CORBIS.

ISBN: 0-7398-9222-3

© 2005 Harcourt Achieve Inc.

10 11 12 13 14 15  1678 17 16 15 14 13 12
4500357489

# Contents

# Exploration and Settlement

This unit is about exploration. You will learn about the different groups of people who explored and settled America. American Indian groups were the first settlers. European explorers came to America later, and European settlers followed.

In this unit, you'll find the answers to questions like these.

- What place did American Indians come from?

- Why did Europeans come to America?

- What kinds of problems did European settlers have as they started new lives in a new land?

## UNIT PROJECT

Start a team project. Choose a group of American Indians and find out how they lived in the past. You can use your findings to show others an American Indian community.

# CHAPTER 1

# The First Americans

Who were the first Americans? How did they get here? In this chapter, you'll find some answers to these questions. You'll learn about different groups of American Indians, also called Native Americans. You'll discover what life was like long ago in America.

## Getting to America

Imagine what it would be like if the land were covered with snow and ice as far as you could see. Thousands of years ago, during the Ice Age, great sheets of ice called **glaciers** covered much of the land. As the ice sheets grew, they drew water from the oceans. This made the oceans shrink. Some land once covered by water was now above water.

 **Write a short weather report for a day during the Ice Age.**

the weather was colled

American Indians were the first people to live in America.

6

There was now land above the water between Asia and North America. The land that connected Asia to North America was like a bridge. Find this land bridge on the map below.

Plants began to grow on the land bridge. Soon animals from Asia went there to eat the plants. They ate their way across the land bridge from Asia to America. Next, small groups of hunters crossed the land bridge. The hunters were following the animals. Finally, after thousands of years, some groups reached as far south as the southern tip of South America.

For hundreds of years, hunters continued to cross the land bridge. They were the first people to reach North America. These people were the first Americans. They were the **ancestors** of the American Indians of today. Ancestors are parents, grandparents, and the people who came before them.

**Look at the map below. With your pencil, trace the longest route that the early hunters followed. It should begin in Asia and end in South America.**

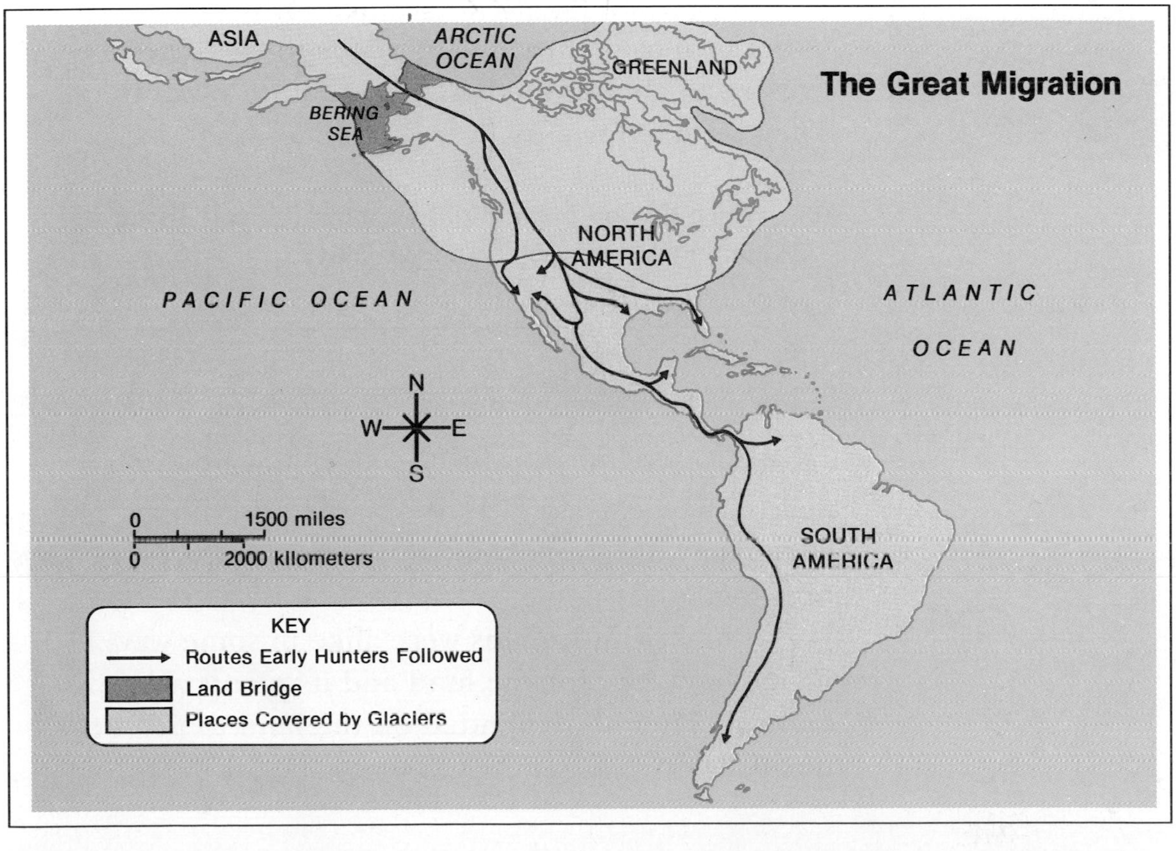
The Great Migration
ASIA
ARCTIC OCEAN
GREENLAND
BERING SEA
NORTH AMERICA
PACIFIC OCEAN
ATLANTIC OCEAN
N
W
E
S
0 1500 miles
0 2000 kilometers
SOUTH AMERICA
KEY
Routes Early Hunters Followed
Land Bridge
Places Covered by Glaciers

(right) American Indians dried corn in the sun so the corn would keep. They ate the dried corn in the winter when food was harder to get. (below) American Indians were very skilled at hunting deer.

## People of the Americas

After many thousands of years, the glaciers melted. The water in the sea rose. Once again, the land bridge was covered by the sea. By then, people were living in all parts of North and South America.

American Indians had to learn new ways to get food in the new lands. How they got food depended on where they lived. People who lived near rivers or lakes or along the coast learned to fish for their food. In other places, people continued to hunt animals. Other groups gathered wild plants to eat. They learned to choose the best seeds and to plant them. They became farmers.

 **Which do you think might be more difficult, living by hunting or living by farming? Why?**

_____

_____

Slowly, American Indian groups moved farther apart. They learned different ways to do things. There were many different American Indian **cultures,** or ways of living.

All American Indians were alike in some ways. All had a great love for the land and its plants and animals. They all depended on the land to meet their needs.

# Culture Regions of the United States

American Indians lived all over what is now the United States. Each group had to find the best way to live in its own area. For example, knowing how to build canoes was important in the lake regions. In the desert, it was more important to know how to save water.

The map on this page shows five different regions of the United States. It also shows the names of some groups of American Indians that lived in each region. Groups that lived in the same region often had similar cultures.

 **Look at the map below. Circle the names of the five regions. Find your region. List two American Indian groups that once lived in your region.**

_____

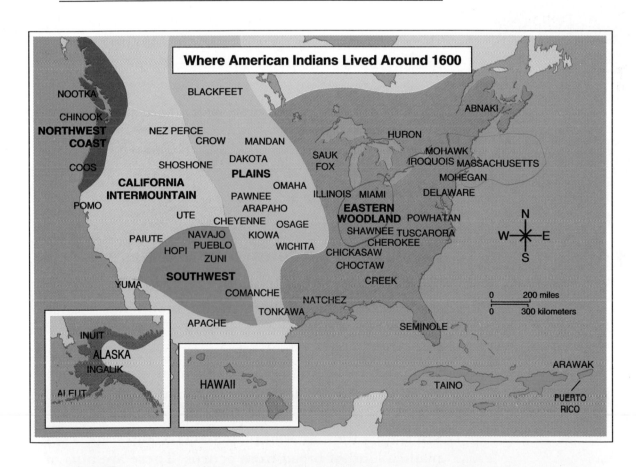

**Where American Indians Lived Around 1600**

NOOTKA
BLACKFEET
ABNAKI
CHINOOK
**NORTHWEST COAST**
NEZ PERCE
HURON
CROW  MANDAN
MOHAWK
IROQUOIS MASSACHUSETTS
SAUK
FOX
DAKOTA
COOS
SHOSHONE
**PLAINS**
MOHEGAN
**CALIFORNIA**
OMAHA
ILLINOIS MIAMI
DELAWARE
**INTERMOUNTAIN**
PAWNEE
POMO
ARAPAHO
**EASTERN**
UTE
**WOODLAND** POWHATAN
CHEYENNE  OSAGE
SHAWNEE TUSCARORA
PAIUTE
NAVAJO  KIOWA
CHEROKEE
HOPI  PUEBLO
WICHITA
CHICKASAW
ZUNI
CHOCTAW
**SOUTHWEST**
YUMA
CREEK
COMANCHE
NATCHEZ
TONKAWA
APACHE
SEMINOLE

N
W—E
S

0  200 miles
0  300 kilometers

INUIT
**ALASKA**
INGALIK
ALEUT

HAWAII

ARAWAK

TAINO

PUERTO RICO

 **UNIT PROJECT Tip** With your team, choose one of the American Indian groups shown on the map on this page. Notice the region where the group lived. Find out about the group's culture. Did the people fish, farm, or hunt?

9

## The Northwest Coast Region

American Indians who lived in the Northwest Coast Region got so much food from the sea and land that they did not need to farm. They caught many kinds of fish and shellfish in the waters near the coast. They also collected nuts, berries, and other plants for food.

The Northwest Coast Region also has thick forests. American Indians used the trees of the forest to make tools, boxes, houses, and canoes. They took these canoes out into the ocean to hunt seals. They also hunted for animals in the forests. These groups were lucky because the region has a mild **climate.** Climate is the kind of weather an area has over a long period of time. The Northwest Coast Region has cool summers, cold winters, and it gets a lot of rain.

Part of a group's culture has to do with the group's beliefs. The American Indians of the Northwest believed that animal spirits called **totems** protected their families. They carved tall poles showing these animal spirits. The poles are called totem poles.

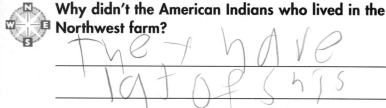

**Why didn't the American Indians who lived in the Northwest farm?**

They have lat of shis

1 → food
shelter

American Indians of the Northwest Coast Region carved colorful totem poles.

## The California Intermountain Region

This region is between two big mountain areas. *Intermountain* means "between the mountains." Much of the land of the region is part of a **basin,** or low place in the land. The land also has many **plateaus,** or high, flat areas. The area is drier than the Northwest Coast Region, because it gets less rain. In dry years the American Indians were often hungry. So they would not starve, they ate wild plants, seeds, and nuts. They made a kind of bread from acorns. These are nuts of the oak tree. They collected food in baskets they made by hand.

American Indians in this region also lived along the coast of California. There, they were able to fish for food.

## The Southwest Region

Many American Indians here belonged to the group known as the Pueblo. The Southwest Region has the driest climate in the country. Much of the region is desert and dry grassland. Instead of using wood, Pueblo buildings were made of **adobe.** Adobe is made of clay, straw, and water. Some villages were a series of rooms built against cliffs.

The Pueblo grew corn, beans, pumpkins, and squash. Since there is so little rainfall in this area, they learned to plant crops near rivers. In some places, they dug ditches to bring the river water to their crops.

**How did the Pueblo grow crops where there is so little rain?**

_____

Two hunters wear wolf skins so they can sneak up on the buffalo.

## The Plains Region

Some American Indians who lived in the Plains Region were both farmers and hunters. The region is flat and grassy. The grassy areas were hard to farm, so most American Indian groups lived in villages near rivers. They planted corn, squash, and beans. They built round houses out of dirt and dried plants. These round houses were called **earth lodges.**

During the summer, some of the people went to hunt for buffalo. They used the buffalo for food. They also made clothing and blankets out of buffalo hides, or skins. While they were hunting, they lived in **tepees,** homes made of buffalo hides.

American Indians of the Southwest Region also lived in hogans. Hogans are usually round, made of earth, and have a single door.

# The Eastern Woodland Region

Look at the map on page 9. Notice that the Eastern Woodland Region is the largest region on the map. It has more than one type of climate. The northern part of the region has warm or hot summers and very cold winters. The southern part of the region has hot summers and mild or warm winters.

Hundreds of years ago, the Eastern Woodland Region was covered with forests. They provided homes for many animals that the American Indians hunted for food. American Indians used wood from the forests to make canoes and tools. People grew corn and other crops and gathered berries. Fish was also an important food. The region has many lakes, and parts of the region are on the Atlantic Ocean.

The American Indians of the Eastern Woodland Region built different kinds of houses depending on the climate. In the northern part of the region, groups such as the Iroquois built **longhouses.** These houses were long wooden buildings with curved roofs. The houses were covered with tree bark to keep out the winter cold. In the southern part of the region, groups such as the Seminole built huts with grass roofs. The sides of the huts were open so that air could be let in to cool the hut.

 **List two natural resources that were important to the American Indians of the Eastern Woodland Region.**

American Indian longhouses ranged from less than 50 feet to more than 200 feet in length. Some longhouses provided shelter for more than ten families.

# Finding Out About the Past

You might be wondering how we know about the American Indians and how they lived hundreds of years ago. One way is by studying **artifacts.** Artifacts are items made by people. They give clues about how people lived. One way scientists find American Indian artifacts is by digging in a place where a community used to be. Some of the artifacts they find include arrowheads, pots, and tools.

The scientists find different kinds of artifacts in different culture regions. The American Indians of the Southwest Region made beautiful pots from clay found in the region. The Northwest Coast American Indians did not make pots. They made beautifully decorated wooden boxes.

 **Why do you think some artifacts from the Northwest Coast are made of wood?**

_tyer wer lotsor free otrso_

Artifacts are not the only way to find out about the past. The American Indians of today keep alive some of the ways of their ancestors. For years parents have told their children stories of what life used to be like. Traditional dances, celebrations, and artwork also provide clues about how the first Americans lived.

(top) This wood and silver pendant was made by the Northwest Coast Indians. It has the raven totem carved on it.

(left) This clay bowl is an artifact from the Southwest Region.

The photograph shows glaciers on an island in the Arctic Ocean, where temperatures rarely get above freezing.

You have already read about a time long ago called the Ice Age. At that time, glaciers, or great sheets of ice, covered much of our land.

Do you know there still are glaciers? Do you know how glaciers are formed? Glaciers form in high mountains and in places where the temperature is always freezing. Each winter it snows a lot. Every year the glaciers get bigger. Layers of snow build up. Most glaciers are from 300 to 10,000 feet thick.

Glaciers are very heavy. The weight of the snow on top turns the snow on the bottom into ice. A glacier becomes so heavy that it starts to move. Glaciers can move even if they are not on a hill. The ice and snow on top slide down the sides. Most glaciers move as slowly as one foot a day. But some glaciers move as fast as 50 feet in one day.

As glaciers move, they pick up rocks and dig up the earth. The glaciers that once covered North America in the Ice Age are gone now. But if you go far enough north you can still see glaciers. Glacier National Park in Montana is named after the 50 glaciers in the park.

 **What causes a glacier to move?**

_____

# CHAPTER ✓ CHECKUP

**Complete each sentence. Circle the letter in front of the correct answer.**

1. The first people who came to America from Asia crossed on a

   a. horse.
   b. land bridge.
   c. ship.
   d. sheet of ice.

2. American Indians from the same region shared the same

   a. forests.
   b. tepee.
   c. houses.
   d. ways of living.

3. American Indians depended on the land for

   a. culture.
   b. food and houses.
   c. tepees and totems.
   d. landforms.

4. The Pueblo of the Southwest Region lived in a

   a. very dry climate.
   b. wet climate.
   c. cold climate.
   d. mild climate.

5. American Indians of the Northwest Coast got most of their food by

   a. fishing and hunting.
   b. farming.
   c. gathering acorns.
   d. carving canoes.

6. Items made by a group of people that give us clues about that group are

   a. longhouses.
   b. totems.
   c. culture.
   d. artifacts.

**THINKING AND WRITING**

American Indians told their children what life used to be like. What other ways can people learn about what life was like in the past?

_____

_____

_____

_____

_____

_____

_____

# Europe in the New World, 982–1664

The first people from Europe reached North America around the year 1000. They were brave sailors.

About 400 years later, other Europeans reached North and South America. They wanted to own new lands across the sea. They wanted to use the natural resources of North and South America to increase their own wealth. In this chapter, you will learn about their exploration of the Americas.

 **Look at the picture on this page. What caused the ships to move?**

WJ Waves

## The Norse Sailors

The Norse, or Northmen, lived in northern Europe in what is now Norway and Sweden. Some people called them Vikings. The Norse were sailors and fighters. Between the years 800 and 1100, they sailed to many lands. Some Norse settled in Iceland.

During the 1400s and 1500s, explorers used the sun and stars to guide them.

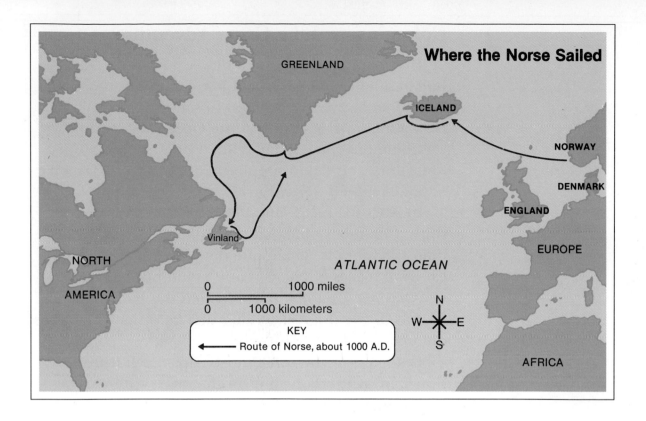

Eric the Red and his son, Leif, were Norse. They were both **explorers.** Explorers travel to unknown places. Eric left Iceland and settled in Greenland. Leif sailed from Greenland to find lands they had never visited. Leif landed in a place he called Vinland. Today, the land he called Vinland is part of Canada, in North America.

 **Look at the map on this page. Look at the distance scale. About how far away is Iceland from Greenland?**

## A New Route to the East?

Stories about the Norse discoveries reached the rest of Europe. But no one paid any attention, so the stories were forgotten. By the 1400s, people in Europe were interested in exploring again. Europeans wanted gold, silk, and spices from Asia. Traders who brought these products to Europe from Asia became rich.

But the journey east to Asia was dangerous. Traders had to cross mountains and deserts. Ships could travel around Africa, but it took a long time. Europeans wanted an easier sea route.

# Columbus and the Great Adventure

How could people find a new sea route to Asia? An Italian sailor named Christopher Columbus thought he had an answer. He wanted to sail west to reach Asia. He wanted to cross the Atlantic Ocean.

Columbus spent many years trying to raise money for sailors, ships, and supplies. Finally, Queen Isabella of Spain agreed to pay for his trip.

In August 1492, Columbus left Spain with three ships. Columbus sailed on the Atlantic Ocean for more than two months. Then, one day the sailors saw birds carrying pieces of plants. Land could not be far away. On October 12, 1492, they reached the Bahama Islands. It was not Asia at all, but a land that Columbus did not even know was there.

Columbus made three more trips. Each trip route is shown in a different color on the map. With your finger, trace each trip.

**Look at the routes again. In which year did Columbus reach South America?**

1498

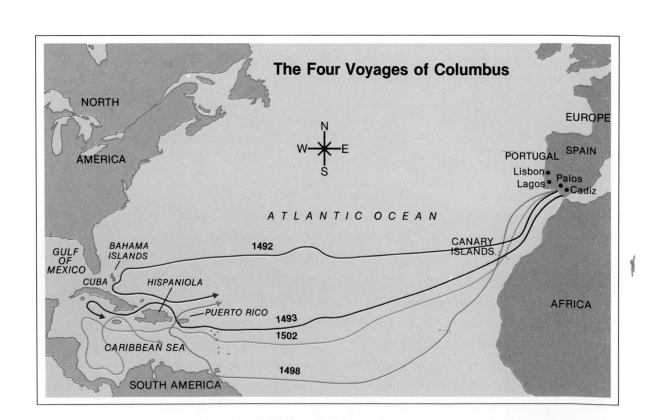

The Four Voyages of Columbus

NORTH AMERICA
EUROPE
SPAIN
PORTUGAL
Lisbon
Lagos
Palos
Cadiz
ATLANTIC OCEAN
GULF OF MEXICO
BAHAMA ISLANDS
CANARY ISLANDS
1492
CUBA
HISPANIOLA
PUERTO RICO
1493
1502
CARIBBEAN SEA
1498
AFRICA
SOUTH AMERICA

# Spanish Explorers in the Americas

Columbus did not know where he had sailed. He thought that he had reached a part of Asia. He did not find a sea route for traders, but Spain became rich anyway. Other people from Spain soon went to the lands that Columbus had reached.

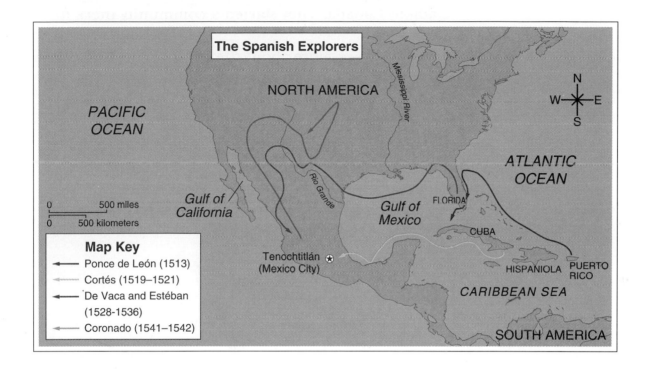

 In 1513, a Spanish explorer reached land that is now part of the United States. He sailed to Florida. On the map, circle the name of the island he sailed from. What was the explorer's name?

_____

In 1519, the Spanish explorer Hernando Cortés sailed to what is now Mexico. Cortés and his men were searching for gold. They found the rich **empire** of a group of American Indians we call the Aztecs. An empire is a group of lands under one ruler. The ruler of the Aztec empire was Montezuma.

At first the Aztecs did not try to fight Cortés. They believed that a great god would come to their land. Montezuma thought Cortés might be that god. He welcomed Cortés to his lands, but Cortés put him in prison. Then Cortés claimed the Aztec land for Spain.

# Other Europeans in the Americas

In 1497, England sent an Italian sailor named John Cabot across the Atlantic Ocean. Cabot found rich fishing grounds near Canada. That gave England a claim to Canada. In 1535, the French explorer Jacques Cartier sailed up the river we call the St. Lawrence. He was looking for a route to Asia. That gave the French a claim to Canada. They started a community there in 1608.

You can see more about the dates of these events in the chart and the **time line** below. A time line is a diagram that shows a period of time. The time line below shows a period of seven **centuries,** or 700 years. It shows when some of the early explorers traveled to places in North America.

 **Find Cortés on the chart of explorers below. Mark the date of his trip on the time line.**

**TIME LINE OF EXPLORERS**

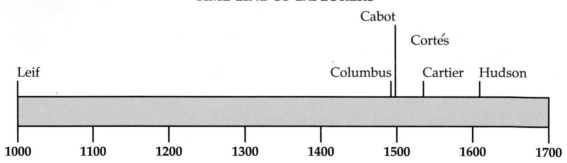

**EXPLORERS OF NORTH AMERICA**

| Explorer | Date of Trip | Country Sent By | Explorer | Date of Trip | Country Sent By |
|----------|--------------|-----------------|----------|--------------|-----------------|
| Leif | 1000 | Norway | de Vaca & Estéban | 1528 | Spain |
| Columbus | 1492 | Spain | Cartier | 1535 | France |
| Cabot | 1497 | England | Coronado | 1541 | Spain |
| de León | 1513 | Spain | Champlain | 1608 | France |
| Cortés | 1519 | Spain | Hudson | 1609 | Netherlands |

UNIT PROJECT Tip

Find out what happened when explorers came to lands where your team's American Indian group lived. How did the explorers change the group's way of life?

New Spain, 1650

## New Spain

Spanish people began settling in the Americas in 1493. The map on this page shows the lands that were called New Spain.

 **New Spain was on what two continents?**

_____

Explorers found gold and silver in New Spain. They sent the treasure back to Spain by ship. Sometimes pirates attacked the ships. So the Spanish built a fort in St. Augustine, Florida. Soldiers there protected the ships. St. Augustine was the first European **settlement** in what is now the United States. A settlement is a new place to live. St. Augustine is the oldest city in the United States—it was founded in 1565.

Mexico was the most important part of New Spain. Spanish settlers from Mexico later moved north. They settled in areas that today are Texas, New Mexico, Arizona, and California. They brought their culture, including their language and religion. The Spanish empire grew.

# New France

The French wanted two things in the Americas. They wanted to trap animals for their fur. And they wanted to find a route to the Pacific Ocean.

Two French explorers, Joliet and Marquette, heard about a great river. They thought it might lead to the Pacific Ocean. The great river they found was the Mississippi River.

 **Look at the map on this page. What body of water does the Mississippi River lead to? Could the Mississippi River be a route to the Pacific Ocean?**

Joliet and Marquette did not find the Pacific Ocean. But the French claimed the lands they saw.

The Netherlands also sent an explorer to North America. His name was Henry Hudson. His travels led the Dutch to start an important settlement called New Amsterdam. Today we call that place New York City.

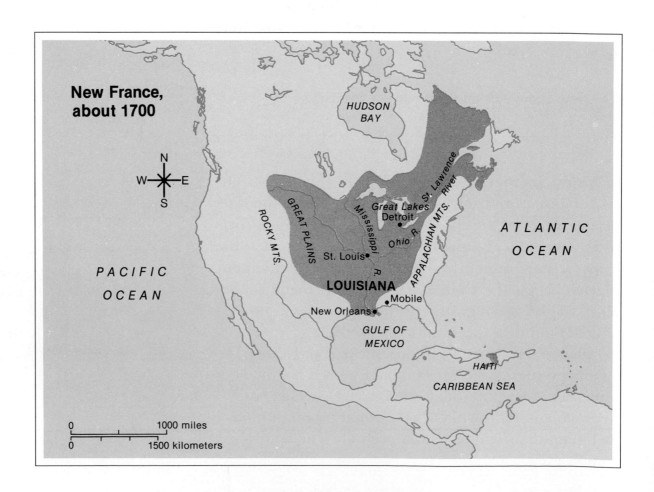

New France, about 1700

HUDSON BAY

ROCKY MTS.

GREAT PLAINS

Great Lakes
Detroit

Mississippi R.

Ohio R.

St. Louis

APPALACHIAN MTS.

St. Lawrence River

ATLANTIC OCEAN

PACIFIC OCEAN

LOUISIANA
Mobile
New Orleans

GULF OF MEXICO

HAITI

CARIBBEAN SEA

0          1000 miles
0          1500 kilometers

Francisco Coronado was one of the Spanish explorers who went to the Americas in search of gold and a new life. In 1535 he sailed to Mexico. Coronado heard stories about a place called Cibola in the American Southwest. People said there were seven cities of gold there. Coronado wanted to find the cities.

Coronado set out to find those cities in 1540. From Mexico he led a small army north. They traveled on foot and on horses. In a few months they found a Zuni American Indian city that seemed to be Cibola. But there was no gold. The city was in what is today New Mexico. Then he led his army farther north to what is now the state of Kansas. But again he found no gold.

**What did Coronado expect to find in Cibola? Write your answer here.**

_____

Coronado and his army returned to Mexico. He had not found what he was looking for. But he had seen the lands of the Southwest Region. He was able to tell the Spanish settlers about the beautiful lands he had seen.

Coronado set out in 1540 to search the American Southwest for cities that were said to be rich in gold. He and his men found American Indian settlements, but they could not find any gold or other riches.

# CHAPTER ✓ CHECKUP

**Complete each sentence. Circle the letter in front of the correct answer.**

1. Norse explorers sailed to
   a. Norway and Florida.
   b. Iceland and Spain.
   c. Canada and Mexico.
   d. Greenland and Vinland.

2. People went to Asia to
   a. get more ships.
   b. become famous.
   c. buy gold, silk, and spices.
   d. find new lands.

3. Columbus hoped to reach Asia
   a. by sailing west.
   b. by sailing east.
   c. by crossing the Pacific Ocean.
   d. by crossing the Caribbean Sea.

4. Hernando Cortés claimed Mexico for
   a. England.
   b. Spain.
   c. Portugal.
   d. France.

5. The country that did not have settlements in North America was
   a. France.
   b. Spain.
   c. England.
   d. Portugal.

6. The French in the Americas wanted to
   a. find gold and silver.
   b. set up farms and ranches.
   c. trap animals for fur.
   d. find Vinland.

**THINKING AND WRITING** Which explorer do you think made the most important achievement? Why do you think so?

_____

_____

_____

_____

_____

_____

_____

_____

_____

_____

# England's First Colonies, 1606–1636

In this chapter, you will read about the first people from England who came to America during the early 1600s. You'll find out why these people came to America. You'll learn where they built their towns. You'll read how they learned to live in a new land.

## The Beginnings of Jamestown

It was a cold December day in 1606. Three small ships carrying about 100 men set sail from London. They were going to start a **colony** in Virginia. A colony is a settlement in one country that is ruled by the government of another country.

An English company sent the men to Virginia to look for gold. They believed they would soon be rich.

The trip to America was long and hard. Many men died. Finally, in May 1607, the men sailed into a river that they called the James River. They built their settlement along the shores of the James River. They called their settlement Jamestown.

The ships that the English colonists sailed in looked like this one.

 **How long did the trip to America take?**

_____

The men built a settlement near a swamp. The water there made many of them sick. Mosquitoes in the swamp carried a sickness that killed some of the **colonists.** Colonists are people who live in a colony.

There were other problems, too. Because they hadn't been farmers in England, the colonists didn't know how to farm. Many of them came from wealthy English families. They were not used to working with their hands. They didn't want to build houses or plant crops. As a result, they didn't have much to eat.

 **What were the Jamestown colonists looking for?**

_____

By 1614, houses were built outside the walls of Jamestown.

## John Smith Helps the Colonists

Things might have been a lot worse for the colonists if it hadn't been for Captain John Smith. He became the leader of the colonists at Jamestown in 1608.

Smith gave clear orders. Anyone who didn't work didn't eat. He made the colonists hunt for food and plant crops. They built houses and a church.

John Smith also made friends with the American Indians. Some American Indians traded with the colonists. Soon the colony began to do well. Soon new colonists came. The colony grew corn and tobacco, and raised pigs.

 **Look at the picture on this page. What things show how the colonists got food?**

 Find out what happened when settlers came to lands where your team's American Indian group lived. How did settlements change the way the group got food?

## The Beginning of Democracy

By 1619, there were 11 small communities near Jamestown. About 1,000 colonists lived in the area.

The English company that ran Jamestown let the colonists share in the government. Each community chose two men. These men were called **burgesses.** They were chosen to meet and make laws for the colonists. This lawmaking group was called the House of Burgesses.

The House of Burgesses made many laws. There were even laws against getting drunk or wasting time.

The House of Burgesses also gave women the right to own property. Most women did not have this right in the early 1600s. But the burgesses knew that the colony would not grow unless both men and women worked hard. What other rules do you think would have been important?

The start of the House of Burgesses was the first step toward **democracy** in America. A democracy is a kind of government in which the people have a say in their laws.

**What did the House of Burgesses do?**

made laws

This is a modern copy of the early colony of Jamestown.

Six years after its start, Plymouth was a busy settlement.

## A Colony at Plymouth

Plymouth, the second English settlement in America, was started because of religion. For years, many people in England disagreed about religion. Many people felt they did not have religious freedom. They wanted to be able to worship in their own way.

One group of people decided to start a colony of their own in America. There they could worship in their own way. We call these people **Pilgrims**. Pilgrims are people who make a trip for religious reasons. In 1620, about 100 men, women, and children sailed from Plymouth, England, in a ship called the *Mayflower*. More than two months later, the Pilgrims landed on the coast of what is now Massachusetts.

 Look at the picture on this page. Take your pencil and follow the road from the bay to the fort. Why do you think the Pilgrims built a fort?

Before leaving the ship, the Pilgrims made an agreement, or **compact.** The Mayflower Compact said that the Pilgrims would work together for everyone's good. They would make rules and follow them.

This agreement was important. It meant that people in America would live under laws they helped make. Like the House of Burgesses, the Mayflower Compact was another step toward democracy.

The Pilgrims were hungry and sick the first winter. But in the spring an American Indian named Squanto came to the colony. He taught the Pilgrims how to grow corn and how to use wild plants for medicine.

That fall, the Pilgrims had lots of food. They decided to celebrate and give thanks. They invited their American Indian friends. It was the first Thanksgiving in America.

**Look at the picture on this page. How are people getting ready for the dinner?**

_____

_____

Pilgrims and American Indians sit down together for the first Thanksgiving dinner.

29

## Massachusetts Bay Colony

While the Plymouth colony was growing, life in England was getting worse. Charles I became king in 1625. Some people known as **Puritans** wanted the king to change the way the English church was run. They were called Puritans because they wanted to make the church simpler, or purer. Charles I refused to listen to their ideas.

In 1630, nearly 1,000 Puritans sailed for Massachusetts. They wanted a better life for themselves in America. They wanted to be able to worship in their own way.

The Puritans did not have as many problems as the Pilgrims did. Some of them were carpenters, teachers, and other people with important skills. They also brought food, clothing, and tools. They started many villages. The most important was Boston.

The Puritan villages chose people to **represent** them, or speak for them. This group, called the **legislature,** made the colony's laws. Like the other English colonists, the people of the Massachusetts Bay Colony shared in their own government.

 **On the map below, circle the three early English colonies.**

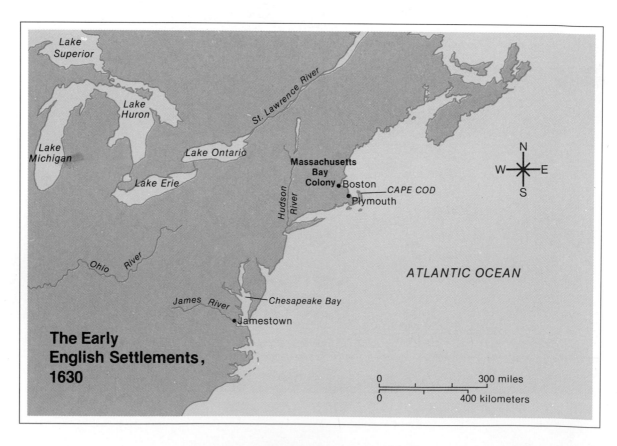

**The Early English Settlements, 1630**

The Puritans left England so they could worship in their own way. In Massachusetts, however, the Puritans didn't allow other people freedom of religion. The colony's laws said that everyone had to go to Puritan churches.

Roger Williams was a Puritan minister who did not think these laws were right. He felt that the church should not be part of the government. Some Puritan leaders tried to send Williams back to England, but he ran away. American Indians helped him and gave him land. Roger Williams and other Puritans started a new town called Providence. Later this area became the colony of Rhode Island.

People of different religious beliefs were welcome in Rhode Island. The idea that people should be free to worship as they please became very important in America.

**In what way were the Puritans not being fair?**

_____

Roger Williams left Massachusetts and started the colony of Rhode Island.

**Complete each sentence. Circle the letter in front of the correct answer.**

1. The colonists of Jamestown were looking for
   a. religious freedom.
   b. gold.
   c. food.
   d. American Indians.

2. John Smith helped the colonists of Jamestown because he was a strong
   a. leader.
   b. carpenter.
   c. fur trader.
   d. boat builder.

3. The House of Burgesses was the first step toward
   a. peace between colonies.
   b. religious freedom.
   c. friendship with American Indians.
   d. democracy.

4. Pilgrims are people who
   a. like to celebrate Thanksgiving.
   b. are friendly with American Indians.
   c. settle in Jamestown.
   d. make a trip for religious reasons.

5. The Massachusetts Bay Colony was settled by
   a. the Puritans.
   b. American Indians.
   c. John Smith.
   d. the Pilgrims.

6. The legislature in the Puritan villages
   a. protected the people.
   b. fished and farmed.
   c. made the laws.
   d. was chosen by Charles I.

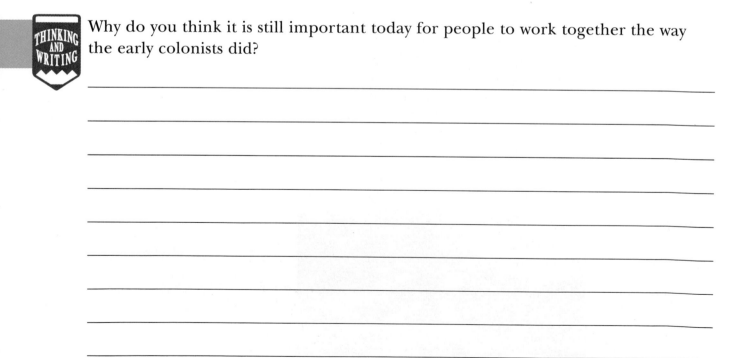

**THINKING AND WRITING** Why do you think it is still important today for people to work together the way the early colonists did?

_____

_____

_____

_____

_____

_____

_____

_____

# Finding Routes on a Map

Since the beginning of time, people have been curious about other places. Long before the Norse sailed to Vinland, people traveled over land and sea in search of new places. Look at the map and map key below.

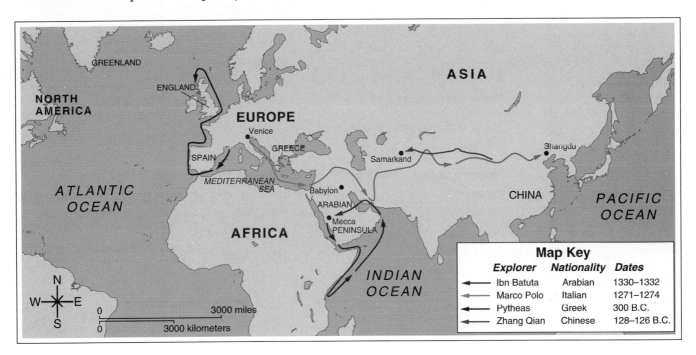

1. The map key tells you which color stands for the route taken by an explorer. It also tells you that explorer's nationality and when he traveled. Which explorer was from China?

   _____

2. Which explorer traveled east from Europe almost all the way across Asia?

   _____

3. Which explorer traveled the farthest south?

   _____

4. Only one of the explorers on the map took a route on the Atlantic Ocean. Which explorer was this?

   _____

5. Is it faster to travel over land or over sea? Why?

   _____

33

Now it's time to finish your unit project. Think about what you learned about the American Indian group you studied. Talk with your team about answers to questions like these.

- **How did the American Indian group use the natural resources of the area?**

- **How did the group's way of life change when European explorers arrived?**

- **What happened when settlers arrived in the area?**

Decide how you want to show others your American Indian community. Choose one of these ways or use one of your own ideas.

➤ Use modeling clay to make your American Indian community. Invite another group to see the community. Show them what a typical day would be like in the community.

➤ Paint a mural of your American Indian community. You may choose to set your mural in a time period after explorers or settlers had come to the area. If so, label items or features in the mural that show the results of the group's contact with others. Display your mural in the classroom.

# The Search for Freedom

This unit tells how the British colonies became the United States of America. You will learn what happened when the colonists finally decided it was time to rule themselves. You will also find the answers to questions like these.

- Where were the 13 colonies?
- Why did the colonists want freedom from Great Britain?
- What happened before they got their freedom?

## UNIT PROJECT

Begin a team project. Imagine your team is starting a new country. Decide what kind of person should lead the country.

# Life in the 13 Colonies, 1650–1750

The small English settlements in Virginia and Massachusetts were only a beginning. By the middle of the 1700s, there were 13 separate English colonies in America.

The colonists were alike in many ways. They were all ruled by Great Britain. Most of them were farmers. They grew their own food and made their own clothes. They had to learn to live with the nearby American Indians.

William Penn was a colonist who made a **treaty** with the American Indians. A treaty is a written agreement. Penn paid them for their land and always treated them fairly.

**In what two ways were the colonists alike?**

_____

_____

In 1681, William Penn made his famous treaty.

The lives of the colonists were different in some ways, too. In this chapter, you will read about the ways of life in the 13 colonies.

# New England Colonies

In 1750 there were four colonies in New England. New England is in the northeast region of the United States. These colonies were Massachusetts, Connecticut, Rhode Island, and New Hampshire.

The biggest city in New England was Boston, Massachusetts. It was a town of pretty brick houses and neat flower gardens. There were several schools and churches in Boston.

Much of the land in New England was rocky and poor. Farming was hard. But off the coast of New England, the ocean waters were filled with fish. Many New Englanders made their living from the ocean. They fished, and they built ships.

Imagine walking around the harbor shown below. You would hear the shouts of the sailors. You would smell fish drying in the open air. Fish were caught by hand and in nets. Then they were cleaned, smoked, or dried with salt. Finally the fish were shipped to Europe to be sold.

**How did many New Englanders make their living?**

_____ Fishing _____

Fishing and building boats were important in New England.

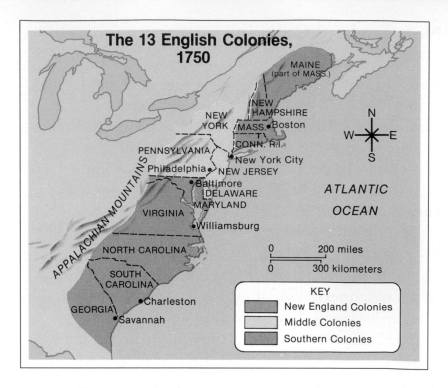

The 13 English Colonies, 1750

KEY
New England Colonies
Middle Colonies
Southern Colonies

## The Middle Colonies

The Middle colonies had rich farmlands. They also had forests full of a small but important animal. This was the beaver. In Europe, beaver hats were popular. Fur trappers and traders became rich selling beaver fur to people in Europe.

 **Look at the map key above. Find the Middle colonies. Write the names of the Middle colonies here.**

_____

_____

William Penn started the colony of Pennsylvania. He said there was to be freedom of religion for all. All men who owned land had the right to vote. Anyone accused of a crime could have a fair trial with a jury.

People came to Pennsylvania from all over Europe. Pennsylvania became a place where many different people lived together in peace.

 UNIT PROJECT Tip

Talk with your team about some of the rules and laws William Penn made for Pennsylvania. Brainstorm a list of laws you would like to have in your team's new country. Name your country.

This painting shows the busy harbor in Philadelphia.

By 1750, Philadelphia, Pennsylvania, was the biggest city in the Middle colonies. A visitor from England wrote, "I had no idea of finding such a place in America. It has nearly 2,000 beautiful brick houses."

The colony of New York grew more slowly. In New York, a few rich people owned much of the land. Workers who lived there could not own the land. So people did not want to settle in New York.

 **Why did New York City grow more slowly than Philadelphia?**

_____

_____

## The Southern Colonies

The five Southern colonies were Maryland, Virginia, North Carolina, South Carolina, and Georgia. In 1750, the one big city was Charleston, South Carolina. Charleston had some of the finest homes in the colonies. Silk and fine china came to Charleston harbor from all over the world.

The Southern colonies were the most **rural.** A rural area is one with many farms and few towns or cities. In the South, large farms were called **plantations.**

A plantation was like a town. It had a vegetable garden and a flour mill. Carpenters, weavers, shoemakers, and blacksmiths lived and worked there.

The main crops were tobacco and rice, which were sold in Northern cities and around the world. Often plantations were built on a river or waterway so goods could travel by water.

Plantations needed many workers. Most colonists wanted their own farms and could buy land cheaply in the western parts of the colonies.

| Why the 13 Colonies Were Settled | | |
|---|---|---|
| **Colony** | **Date Founded** | **Reason Settled** |
| Virginia | 1607 | To carry on trade; chance to build a better life |
| Massachusetts | 1620 | Religious freedom |
| Rhode Island | 1636 | Religious freedom |
| New Hampshire | 1638 | Need for more farmland; religious freedom |
| Connecticut | 1636 | Need for more farmland; religious freedom |
| Delaware | 1638 (Sweden) 1682 (England) | To carry on trade; chance to build a better life |
| Maryland | 1634 | Chance to build a better life; religious freedom |
| New York | 1624 (Netherlands) 1664 (England) | To carry on trade; chance to make money; chance to build a better life |
| New Jersey | 1664 | To carry on trade; chance to make money; chance to build a better life |
| North Carolina | 1670 | To acquire new land and build a better life |
| South Carolina | 1670 | To build a new colony and a better life |
| Pennsylvania | 1682 | Religious freedom |
| Georgia | 1733 | Chance for debtors and the poor to make a new start |

Plantation owners had slaves to work the land. The slaves had been kidnapped from their homes in Africa and brought on ships to America. Here they were bought and sold like pieces of property. By 1750, slaves made up one fourth of the population in the South.

## On the Frontier

The western edge of the 13 colonies was known as the **frontier.** Sometimes small farms there were just cleared places in the woods.

**Look at the picture. After the trees were cut down, what did the people do with them?**

_____

Life was hard for frontier **settlers.** Settlers are people who go to live in a new place. They grew crops like wheat, potatoes, and squash. They hunted for deer and bear. They made most of the things they needed. They baked bread, made jam, spun cloth, and made their own tools.

This frontier settler stands in the doorway of her log cabin.

Some towns still have town meetings today.

Imagine living in a town without a mayor, police department, or firefighters. That's what it was like for colonists living in New England villages. You remember that the government of Great Britain ruled the 13 colonies. But Great Britain was too busy to take care of the matters of small towns in New England. It was up to the colonists to find ways to protect themselves and take care of their small towns.

The men of the village figured out one way to solve these problems. They called a town meeting. Only white men who owned property could vote.

**Who could not vote in New England town meetings?**

_____

_____

At the town meeting, the men voted for the people needed to run the town. For example, they voted for someone to keep the peace, a man to dig graves, and a town crier to give the news.

Today towns, cities, and states all have their own governments and elections. Some towns still have town meetings. People at town meetings might discuss if a town needs a new school or wants to turn some open land into a park. Anyone who lives in the town can come to the meeting. At the town meeting everyone gets a chance to give his or her opinion. Together, people can decide what would be the best plan for the town. Town meetings help people work together for the good of the town.

**What topics might be discussed at a town meeting in your community? Write your answer here.**

_____

_____

# CHAPTER ✓ CHECKUP

**Complete each sentence. Circle the letter in front of the correct answer.**

1. One way in which the colonists were alike was that
   a. they all lived on plantations.
   b. they were all ruled by Great Britain.
   c. they all wore beaver hats.
   d. they all made their living from the ocean.

2. William Penn made a treaty with
   a. the American Indians.
   b. the New Englanders.
   c. the fur trappers.
   d. the colonists from Pennsylvania.

3. The biggest city in New England was
   a. New York City, New York.
   b. Philadelphia, Pennsylvania.
   c. Boston, Massachusetts.
   d. Providence, Rhode Island.

4. Many people settled in Pennsylvania because
   a. they could build log cabins.
   b. they could live on plantations.
   c. they wanted to fish and build ships.
   d. Pennsylvania offered religious freedom.

5. The most important crops grown on Southern plantations were
   a. rice and tobacco.
   b. apples and corn.
   c. wheat and squash.
   d. citrus fruits.

6. Frontier settlers had to
   a. work on plantations.
   b. make most of the things they needed.
   c. go to town meetings.
   d. leave Africa.

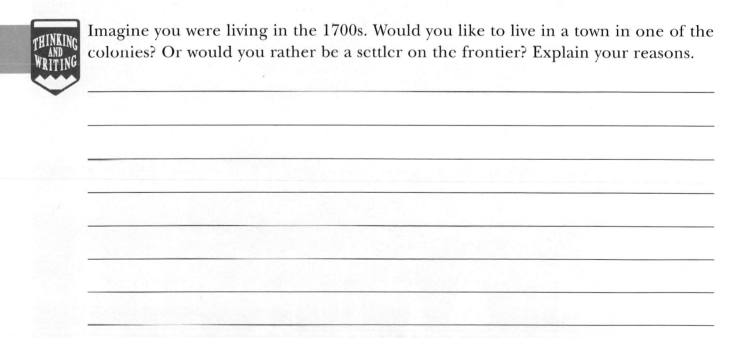

**THINKING AND WRITING** Imagine you were living in the 1700s. Would you like to live in a town in one of the colonies? Or would you rather be a settler on the frontier? Explain your reasons.

_____

_____

_____

_____

_____

_____

# The Road to Freedom, 1750–1776

On July 4 every year, we celebrate Independence Day. This is an important holiday for our nation. On July 4, 1776, the colonists announced that they wanted **independence,** or freedom, from Great Britain. They decided it was time to rule themselves.

The colonists had many reasons to take this step. Over the years the colonists had become angered by Great Britain's treatment of them. In this chapter you will find out why the colonists wanted their freedom. You will also learn why war seemed to be the only way for the colonists to gain independence.

**Why is Independence Day an important holiday?**

_____

_____

Americans like to celebrate the Fourth of July with parades.

# The French and Indian War

France had colonies in Canada and along the Mississippi River. When the British colonists started moving west, the French began to worry. They decided to build forts to protect their colonies. "But," said the British, "some of these forts are built on British land." France and Great Britain began a war that lasted from 1754 to 1763.

In the beginning, the war did not go well for the British. The French had many American Indians fighting on their side. The American Indians didn't want the British colonists to move farther west.

The British government finally sent more soldiers and won the war. In 1763, France and Great Britain agreed to have peace. As a result, Canada and all of North America east of the Mississippi River now belonged to Great Britain.

 Look at the map on this page. What country had the land west of the Mississippi River?

_____

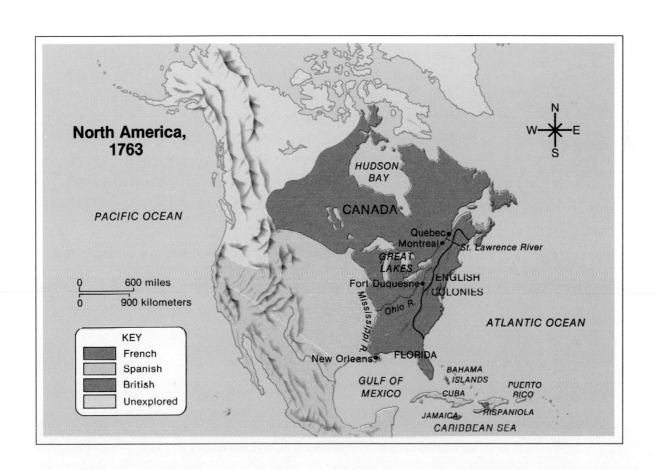

**North America, 1763**

HUDSON BAY

PACIFIC OCEAN

CANADA

Quebec
Montreal
St. Lawrence River

GREAT LAKES

Fort Duquesne

ENGLISH COLONIES

Ohio R.

Mississippi R.

ATLANTIC OCEAN

New Orleans

FLORIDA

GULF OF MEXICO

BAHAMA ISLANDS

PUERTO RICO

CUBA

JAMAICA

HISPANIOLA

CARIBBEAN SEA

0    600 miles
0    900 kilometers

**KEY**
- French
- Spanish
- British
- Unexplored

(top) George III was king of England in 1765. (bottom) Colonists had to pay for tax stamps like this one.

## New Problems

Even though Great Britain won, the French and Indian War cost the British a lot of money. They felt that the colonists should help pay the bills. Britain decided that the colonists would have to pay a **tax** on sugar, molasses, and other goods. A tax is money that people pay for government services.

**Parliament** is the lawmaking group in England. In 1765, it passed a law called the Stamp Act. This law made the colonists buy special stamps for certain goods they bought. The money was used to pay British soldiers in the colonies.

The colonists were already paying taxes to the governments of their colonies. But the Stamp Act was voted for by the Parliament in Great Britain. There were no colonists in Parliament. No one represented them there.

Many colonists spoke out against the Stamp Act. These colonists called themselves the Sons and Daughters of Liberty. England soon **repealed,** or did away with, the Stamp Act because of what the colonists said.

Two years later, Parliament passed another law. This law taxed many goods that the colonists **imported,** or bought from another country. Many colonists **boycotted,** or stopped buying, those goods. The colonists hoped the boycott would make Parliament stop taxing those goods.

The British sent troops to see that the taxes were paid. The soldiers were allowed to search ships, businesses, and even homes. The colonists did not want soldiers in their homes.

**What did many colonists do about the tax on imported goods?**

Talk with your team about the laws Parliament passed. Do you think those laws were fair? How would you make sure everyone was represented in the lawmaking group of your new country?

# The Boston Massacre

The British soldiers and American colonists did not like each other. Sometimes they fought but no one was hurt until March 1770.

A boy and a British soldier in Boston got into an argument. The soldier knocked the boy down. An angry crowd surrounded the soldier. They threw snowballs and yelled at him. Other soldiers ran to help him. Someone yelled "Fire!" The soldiers got scared and fired into the crowd. Five colonists were killed.

These killings came to be called the Boston Massacre. The colonists were very angry. Some colonists passed out small booklets called pamphlets to people in other colonies. The pamphlets told how unfair the British were to Boston colonists. Some of these pamphlets stretched the truth in order to stir up anger among the colonists against the British.

**Which groups made up the two sides in the Boston Massacre?**

_____

This picture of the Boston Massacre shows British troops firing on a crowd of helpless colonists. The picture does not show that the colonists threw snowballs at the soldiers first. This picture is an example of how the colonists sometimes stretched the truth about events between the colonists and the British.

The Boston Tea Party was a protest against the tea tax.

## The Boston Tea Party

As a result of the Boston Massacre, Parliament ended all the taxes the colonists hated—except one. That tax was on tea.

People all over the colonies refused to pay this tax. They stopped buying and drinking tea. Then, on the night of December 16, 1773, a group of colonists boarded a British ship in Boston Harbor. They dumped more than 300 chests of tea into the water. This event is now called the Boston Tea Party.

The "tea party" made the British very angry. They wanted the colonists to pay for the ruined tea. Parliament passed several laws that hurt the colonists. One law closed Boston Harbor. No ships could come or go from the harbor. Another law said British soldiers could live in the homes of the colonists.

These laws made the colonists begin to think about breaking away from Great Britain and starting their own country. They saw that they would probably have to fight for their freedom.

**What effect do you think closing the harbor had on the Boston colonists?**

# Events That Led to War

In September 1774, some colonial leaders met in Philadelphia. This meeting was called the First Continental Congress. The leaders decided to write to the British king to ask him to change the tax laws.

At the same time, colonists in Boston were planning to protect themselves. An army of farmers and store owners was formed to fight the British. They would be ready at a minute's notice. Proudly, they called themselves the Minutemen.

The British soldiers in Boston heard that the colonists were storing gunpowder in the town of Concord. On April 18, 1775, British soldiers left Boston to get the gunpowder. Two colonists, Paul Revere and William Dawes, secretly left Boston on horseback to warn the Minutemen. When the British arrived in Lexington on their way to Concord, the Minutemen were waiting for them.

The first shots of the American Revolution were fired, and eight colonists were killed. The British pushed on to Concord, but they did not find gunpowder. The colonists had taken it away. As the British marched back to Boston, Minutemen fought them all the way.

 **Look at the battle map below. It shows where battles took place. Battle maps can help you figure out the events of a war. Circle where two early battles of the American Revolution took place.**

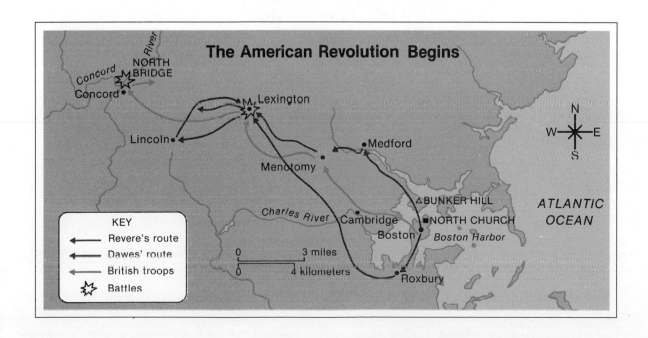

The American Revolution Begins

KEY
← Revere's route
← Dawes' route
← British troops
✫ Battles

# The Call for Independence

News of what had happened at Lexington and Concord spread throughout the colonies. Two months later there was another important battle called the Battle of Bunker Hill.

The colonists who fought were not professional soldiers like the British. They were mostly farmers who had not had any army training. At the Battle of Bunker Hill, the colonists fought bravely against the British until they ran out of gunpowder. Although the British won, the colonists had fought very well. The colonists had killed almost half of the British soldiers who fought during the battle.

In Philadelphia, the Second Continental Congress met in May 1775. They decided the colonies needed a regular army. The Congress had to figure out how to train soldiers and pay for war supplies. They made George Washington the **commander,** or leader, of the new Continental Army.

A year later the leaders of the Continental Congress asked Thomas Jefferson and others to write a statement. It was to declare, or tell, that the colonies were breaking away from Great Britain, and why. It told Great Britain that the colonies wanted to become their own country. It was called the Declaration of Independence. The declaration was read aloud to the colonists on July 4, 1776.

Look at the time line below. Write *Declaration of Independence* where it belongs on the time line.

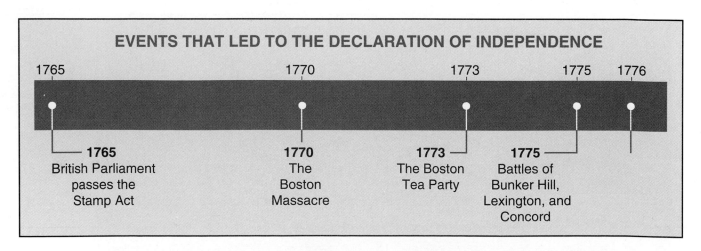

## EVENTS THAT LED TO THE DECLARATION OF INDEPENDENCE

1765   1770   1773   1775   1776

**1765**
British Parliament passes the Stamp Act

**1770**
The Boston Massacre

**1773**
The Boston Tea Party

**1775**
Battles of Bunker Hill, Lexington, and Concord

50

Until the Declaration of Independence was written, not all colonists were sure they wanted independence. Some just wanted the British to stop passing laws that were unfair to the colonies. Early in 1776, a colonist named Thomas Paine wrote a pamphlet called *Common Sense*. In it, he gave reasons for independence. Many colonists decided to fight for independence because Thomas Paine's reasons were so good.

The Declaration of Independence has become one of the most important statements in the world. It is about the rights and freedoms that all people should have. One of its most famous lines states that everyone should have the right to "life, liberty, and the pursuit of happiness."

**What did the Declaration of Independence tell Great Britain?**

_____

_____

(above) Thomas Jefferson (below) Thomas Jefferson wrote most of the Declaration of Independence.

Abigail and John Adams

"Alas! You are 300 miles from home. How many snow banks divide us. And my warmest wishes to see you will not melt one of them."

Abigail Adams wrote this to her husband, John. We know a lot about John and Abigail Adams because of the letters they wrote to each other. John Adams was a colonial leader. When Abigail wrote this note in 1774, John was meeting with the First Continental Congress in Philadelphia. Later he was one of the men who signed the Declaration of Independence. Still later he became the second President of the United States of America.

While John was away, Abigail had a lot to do at their home in Massachusetts. She managed the farm, raised the children, and ran the house.

In colonial times, women were not supposed to have jobs outside the home. Colonial women were expected to stay home with the children. Abigail, like many other women, taught her daughters. Her sons went away to school. Abigail Adams accepted this, but she did not think it was fair.

Abigail Adams hoped that the First Continental Congress would decide to break away from Great Britain. Then Americans could make their own laws. Again she wrote to her husband.

"And in the new laws which you will make, I wish you would remember the ladies. Be more favorable and generous to them than your ancestors. Do not put so much power in the hands of husbands."

Abigail acted and thought for herself. Both John and Abigail Adams were leaders in the fight for independence.

**What did Abigail Adams think was not fair?**

_____

_____

# CHAPTER ✓ CHECKUP

**Complete each sentence. Circle the letter in front of the correct answer.**

1. Independence Day celebrates
   a. the winning of the French and Indian War.
   b. the lawmaking group in England.
   c. the Boston Massacre.
   d. the colonists' decision to declare their freedom from Great Britain.

2. The French and Indian War ended in
   a. 1766.
   b. 1775.
   c. 1763.
   d. 1773.

3. To show how they felt about taxes on imported goods, the colonists
   a. passed a tax on these goods.
   b. paid a lot of money for these goods.
   c. made sure the taxes were paid.
   d. stopped buying these goods.

4. The Minutemen were
   a. British soldiers.
   b. colonists.
   c. American Indians.
   d. trained professional soldiers.

5. The Second Continental Congress wanted a statement declaring independence written by
   a. John Adams.
   b. The Sons and Daughters of Liberty.
   c. King George.
   d. Thomas Jefferson.

6. The Declaration of Independence is about
   a. the rights and freedoms that all people should have.
   b. finding a way to pay for war supplies.
   c. problems in Great Britain.
   d. the members of the Continental Congress.

**THINKING AND WRITING**

Why didn't the colonists want to pay taxes passed by Parliament?

_____

_____

_____

_____

_____

_____

_____

# The American Revolution, 1776–1783

In the last chapter, you read about the events leading up to the Declaration of Independence. Americans had to fight for freedom from Great Britain. In this chapter you will read how the American Revolution was fought. You will also read about the important people who made **victory** possible. Victory is the defeat of an enemy.

 **Why were many Americans willing to fight the British in the American Revolution?**

The Battle of Bunker Hill was one of the first battles of the American Revolution.

# The Long Fight

Not all Americans wanted the Revolution. Some people remained **loyal,** or faithful, to Great Britain. They were called **Loyalists.** The people who were for independence called themselves **Patriots.** The Patriots fought the battles that won the American Revolution.

The British thought it would be easy to win the war. They had an army of trained soldiers. They also paid professional German soldiers to fight on their side. The British did not think the Americans were very good soldiers. For two years, the British Army chased General Washington and his soldiers. But even though the Continental Army lost many battles, they always escaped from the enemy.

## Washington and the American Army

General Washington had a hard time taking care of his men. A lot of them did not have **uniforms,** or special army clothes. So they wore their regular clothes. Some soldiers had to fight and march without shoes. Many of them had no blankets or tents. During the cold weather, some men got sick and died. There wasn't always enough food. Many soldiers went hungry.

Unlike the British Army, the American Army was not trained to be soldiers. Most of the men were farmers, fishermen, and store owners who were not used to taking orders from an army commander. Some would only fight in battles near their homes. Others left the army when it was time to plant or harvest crops. So Washington had a hard job keeping the army together.

But Washington was a good leader. His men trusted and respected him. Because of this, Washington was able to keep the army going.

This is an example of the uniforms worn by the British Army during the American Revolution.

**List two problems the American Army had.**

_____

_____

George Washington became the first President of the United States. With your group talk and take notes about the qualities that make a good leader of a country.

## The Victory at Trenton

It was December 1776. General Washington had only about 2,500 men left in his army. Many soldiers were sick and didn't have warm clothes. Americans were beginning to lose hope.

Finally something good happened. On Christmas Eve, Washington had a plan.

It was a very cold night. Washington led his army across the Delaware River in boats. Then the cold and tired men marched to Trenton, New Jersey. There was a camp of German soldiers in Trenton. They were celebrating Christmas. They had no idea Washington was coming!

Washington's soldiers surprised the Germans and captured their camp. They took more than 900 German prisoners.

The victory at Trenton made Americans feel more hopeful about winning the war. So more men signed up to fight. The British Army, however, was still stronger than the American Army.

**Why did the battle at Trenton give Americans hope?**

_____

_____

George Washington leads his men into battle.

The Marquis de Lafayette (on the left) meets George Washington.

## Help Arrives from Europe

While Washington worked to keep his army together, other colonial leaders were trying to get help. Benjamin Franklin tried to get France to enter the war on the side of the Americans. Great Britain and France were old enemies. So the Americans thought France might fight with them.

The French entered the war after the American victory at Saratoga, New York, in 1777. This victory let the French know that the Americans were strong.

One rich Frenchman had already joined the Patriots. He was the Marquis de Lafayette. He arrived in America with other French soldiers in June 1777. He offered to serve in the American Army as a regular soldier. Instead, the Continental Congress made him a leader. Lafayette was only 20 years old when he joined the Americans.

Help came from other European nations, too. Germany and Poland sent men who were good army leaders. They helped train the American soldiers. Some countries also gave the Americans money.

**What European countries helped the Patriots?**

_____

_____

General Washington and the Marquis de Lafayette at Valley Forge during the winter of 1777–78.

Baron Friedrich von Steuben helped train American soldiers.

## Winter at Valley Forge

The British Army was spending a comfortable winter in Philadelphia. But the winter of 1777 was very hard for Washington and his men. They camped on a frozen plain in Pennsylvania called Valley Forge. The soldiers were often hungry. Many men were sick that winter, too. Their shoes, if they had any, were worn out. Washington wrote, "You could tell where the army had been by the blood of their feet on the snow."

In these hard times, a soldier came to the Patriot camp to help. His name was Baron Friedrich von Steuben. He was from Prussia, a country in Europe known for its strong army. George Washington asked von Steuben to teach his soldiers how to fight better.

The Patriots were brave, but they did not know how to fight in an organized way. They were used to hiding in the forests and making surprise attacks. Now they had to fight the British on open fields. Von Steuben taught the American soldiers how to fight together as a group.

**What were conditions like for the soldiers at Valley Forge?**

## Charleston Falls to the British

In the spring of 1780, the British captured the important port city of Charleston, South Carolina. There they captured many American soldiers. It was the biggest British victory of the war.

The British had control of the Charleston port and of several other important cities. But they couldn't win the war. America was too big. Look at the map below. Battles took place all over. The British couldn't stop the Patriots in all the small towns and villages.

Small groups of Patriots captured British supplies. They made surprise attacks. One fighter known for surprise attacks was Francis Marion of South Carolina. His nickname was the "Swamp Fox." He got his name because the British could never catch him.

 **Look at the map. In which colonies were the battles of Saratoga, Trenton, and Charleston fought?**

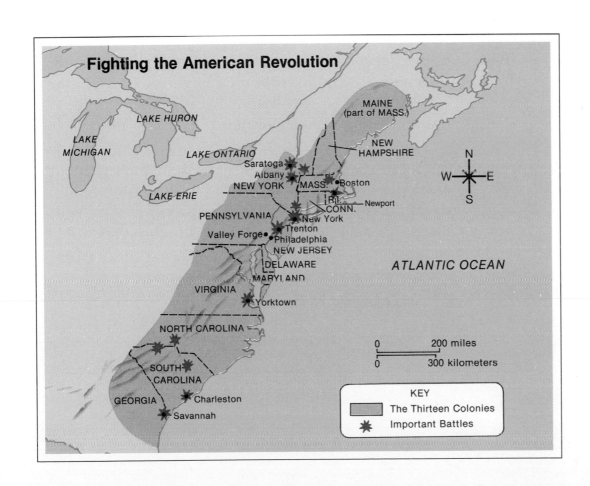

Fighting the American Revolution

LAKE HURON

LAKE MICHIGAN

LAKE ONTARIO

MAINE (part of MASS.)

NEW HAMPSHIRE

Saratoga
Albany
NEW YORK    MASS.    •Boston
LAKE ERIE
R.I.
CONN.    — Newport
PENNSYLVANIA    •New York
Trenton
Valley Forge•    •Philadelphia
NEW JERSEY
DELAWARE
MARYLAND
VIRGINIA
Yorktown
NORTH CAROLINA

ATLANTIC OCEAN

0    200 miles
0    300 kilometers

SOUTH CAROLINA
GEORGIA    •Charleston
Savannah

KEY
The Thirteen Colonies
★ Important Battles

## Another Kind of Fight for Freedom

The Declaration of Independence is about the rights and freedoms that all people should have. But not everyone was equal. Women did not have the same rights as white men, and most African Americans were slaves.

During the American Revolution, some slaves were promised freedom if they would fight against the British. Rhode Island even passed a law that said every slave who would fight for the Patriots would be free. Rhode Island formed a Patriot **regiment,** or team of soldiers, made up mostly of African Americans.

In Newport, Rhode Island, the Rhode Island regiment fought against a regiment of well-trained Germans. The Germans yelled at the African American soldiers and ran at them pointing sharp **bayonets.** A bayonet is a piece of pointed metal placed on the end of a rifle. A soldier could stab and kill someone with a bayonet.

The African Americans in the Rhode Island regiment fought bravely. Even though the African Americans had no uniforms or bayonets, they killed many of the German soldiers. The Patriots won the Battle of Newport. The day after the battle, the leader of the German soldiers asked to be moved to another regiment. He said his own men might shoot him if he led them into another battle! They blamed him for losing so many men at Newport.

Many other African Americans fought for freedom during the American Revolution. After the Revolution, many slave owners in the North began to free their slaves. But in the South, African Americans were still slaves. It would be almost 100 years before they would be free.

This is a painting of a battle during the American Revolution.

**What law did Rhode Island pass?**

_____

_____

# The Last Battle: Yorktown

British General Cornwallis marched his armies toward Yorktown, on the coast of Virginia. French soldiers had joined Washington's army. The Americans and the French set out after the British. At Yorktown, the British were trapped. The French Navy blocked Cornwallis from the sea. American and French forces kept Cornwallis from escaping on land.

Cornwallis knew he had lost. He surrendered on October 19, 1781. The American Revolution was over. The 13 colonies had finally won their independence from Great Britain. In 1783, Great Britain and the new United States signed a peace treaty.

 **Look at the map. After 1783, what nation owned most of the land east of the Mississippi River?**

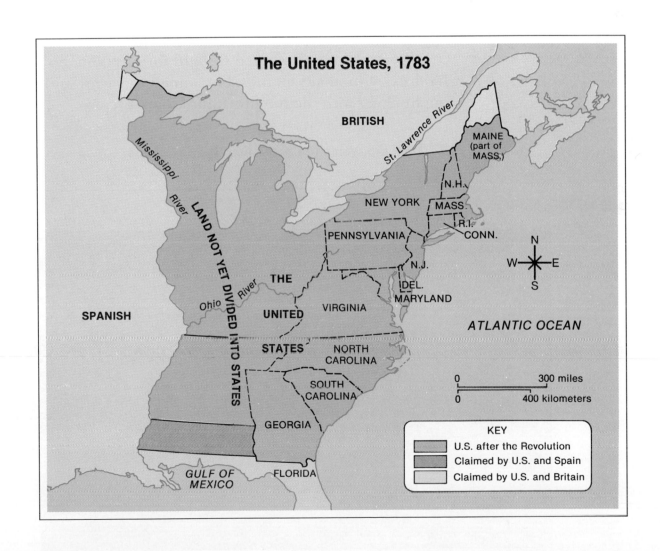

**The United States, 1783**

BRITISH

St. Lawrence River

MAINE (part of MASS.)

N.H.

NEW YORK

MASS.

R.I.

CONN.

Mississippi River

LAND NOT YET DIVIDED INTO STATES

PENNSYLVANIA

N.J.

DEL.

MARYLAND

THE

Ohio River

SPANISH

UNITED

VIRGINIA

ATLANTIC OCEAN

STATES

NORTH CAROLINA

SOUTH CAROLINA

0    300 miles
0    400 kilometers

GEORGIA

GULF OF MEXICO

FLORIDA

**KEY**
| | |
|---|---|
| | U.S. after the Revolution |
| | Claimed by U.S. and Spain |
| | Claimed by U.S. and Britain |

# Women in the Revolution

The American Revolution was not won only by men. Women, too, helped make victory possible.

While men were away fighting, women did all the work the men had done. They farmed so that their families and the soldiers would have food. They had to cook, clean, sew, and take care of children. Women also made guns and supplies for the soldiers. A woman known as "Handy Betsy the Blacksmith" was famous for all the cannons and guns she made.

Although rules said that women weren't allowed to fight in the battles, women did go to the battlefront. Many women served as nurses and cooks. George Washington's wife often helped at the battlefront.

Mary Hays brought food and water to soldiers. They called her Molly Pitcher because she brought pitchers of water. When her husband was hit by a bullet, Molly Pitcher ran to take his place.

Deborah Sampson wanted to fight for freedom. So she dressed in men's clothes. She joined the army and fought along with the men for more than a year.

**How did women at home help the revolution?**

_____

Molly Pitcher fought for freedom.

# CHAPTER CHECKUP

**Complete each sentence. Circle the letter in front of the correct answer.**

1. Patriots were people who
   a. were loyal to the king.
   b. fought on the British side.
   c. fought for American independence.
   d. did not want independence.

2. The leader of the Continental Army was
   a. Benjamin Franklin.
   b. Francis Marion.
   c. George Washington.
   d. General Cornwallis.

3. French soldiers fought on the side of
   a. the British.
   b. the Germans.
   c. the Loyalists.
   d. the Patriots.

4. Von Steuben helped train the American soldiers to
   a. fight together as a group.
   b. fight from behind trees.
   c. use ships in battle.
   d. make surprise attacks.

5. The Battle of Newport was won
   a. with the help of German soldiers.
   b. with the help of French soldiers.
   c. with the help of an African American regiment.
   d. because General Cornwallis surrendered.

6. After the war, the land that made up the United States included
   a. all of Canada.
   b. land east of the Mississippi River.
   c. land west of the Mississippi River.
   d. land south of the Mississippi River.

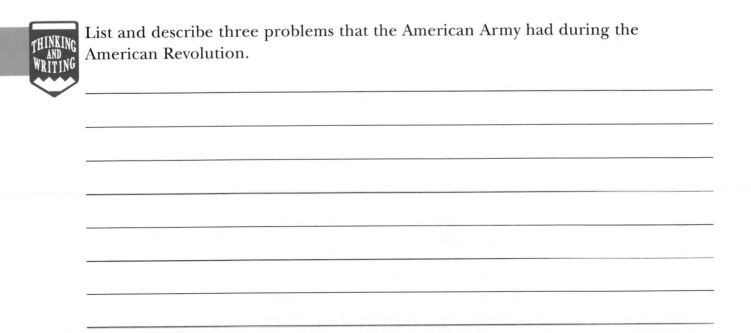

**THINKING AND WRITING** List and describe three problems that the American Army had during the American Revolution.

_____

_____

_____

_____

_____

_____

_____

# Unit 2 Skill Builder
## Reading a Battle Map

The French and Indian War began in 1754 after the French built forts on land the British said belonged to them. The French had American Indians fighting with them. On the other side were the British and American colonists. Look at the battle map below.

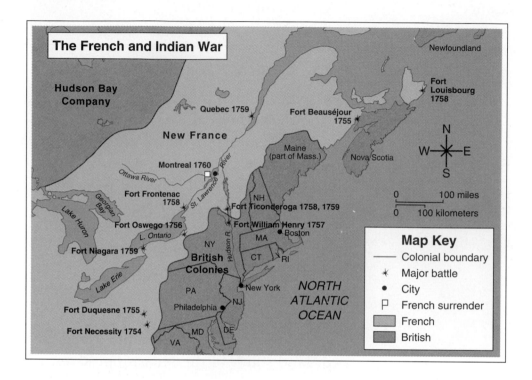

1. George Washington fought on the British side in the first battle of the war. Write the name and date of the first battle here.

2. Were most battles fought on land claimed by the French or by the British?

3. In 1758 the British Navy sailed to Fort Louisbourg and took over the fort. Circle Fort Louisbourg.

4. After taking Fort Louisbourg, the British sailed down the St. Lawrence River and defeated the French in the Battle of Quebec. Trace the British route from Fort Louisbourg to Quebec.

Now it's time to finish your unit project. Think about what you learned about starting a new country. Talk with your team about questions like these.

- **What kinds of laws do you think a new country should have?**

- **How can you make sure everyone has a voice in making the laws?**

- **What qualities should a leader have?**

Decide how you want to show the results of your project. Choose one of these ways or use one of your own ideas.

➤ With your team, write a Declaration of Independence based on your ideas about rules and laws, fairness, and good leadership. Choose one of your team members to be a presidential candidate. Have the candidate give a speech to your class about the new country and why he or she would be the right person to lead the country. After all the teams' candidates have given their speeches, take a vote.

➤ Use the ideas your team brainstormed about rules and laws, fairness, and good leadership to make a poster for the President of your new country. Display the posters in the classroom. Write your vote on a slip of paper and place it in a ballot box.

# From Sea to Shining Sea

America had fought hard for independence. Now the United States had to work to make a new government. This unit will tell you how our country grew. You will learn what happened as settlers moved west beyond the original 13 states.

In this unit, you'll find the answers to questions like these.

- What kind of government was created after the Revolution?

- What was the Louisiana Purchase?

- How did the map of the United States change between the years 1783 and 1853?

## UNIT PROJECT

Imagine you and your team are a family living in Philadelphia in 1783. As the land to the west opens up, your family decides to go west and become pioneers. Each member of your team should take the role of one family member. Keep a journal of what you see and do on your way west.

# The New Nation, 1783–1800

America had won its independence. Now the Americans had to form a government that would keep them free. In this chapter, you'll learn about this new government and how it was set up.

## The Articles of Confederation

During the war, the colonies agreed to make up a group of rules. These rules were called the Articles of Confederation. The Articles set up **Congress,** a group that makes laws, to help govern the nation.

**What were the rules that the colonies made called?**

_____

George Washington led the group that discussed the new government.

Benjamin Franklin (above) and James Madison (below) were important delegates at the Philadelphia meeting where the Constitution was written.

## The New Nation Faces Problems

The new Congress was not very strong, but most Americans liked that. They had had enough strong government under the British. On the other hand, the new nation faced problems that the weak Congress could not solve.

For example, Congress could not pass taxes. It could only ask each state to pay its share of running the government. The states also fought with one another over boundary lines. Courts in one state could not settle arguments of another state. People went on thinking of themselves as New Yorkers or Virginians, not as Americans.

The powerful European countries didn't take the new nation seriously. When John Adams was in Great Britain trying to set up trade agreements, he was asked, "Do you represent one nation or thirteen?"

Several American leaders became worried. How could such a weak government protect the nation? Could the nation even continue? The leaders decided to meet in May 1787 to discuss these problems.

## A New Plan of Government

At the meeting in Philadelphia, there were 55 **delegates.** Delegates were people chosen to represent and speak for all Americans. Some delegates hoped simply to change the Articles of Confederation. But they soon realized that this would not be enough. The delegates agreed to start over and make a new government.

The delegates worked six days a week for four months. On September 17, 1787, only one job was left. Each delegate signed the **constitution.** A constitution is a group of laws. The United States Constitution is the basic law of our land.

**Why were people glad that the Congress set up by the Articles of Confederation was not strong?**

_____

_____

The Constitution was signed on September 17, 1787, at Independence Hall in Philadelphia, Pennsylvania.

## A New Law for a New Land

While writing the Constitution, the delegates often disagreed with one another. One disagreement was about how to set up the legislature. The delegates wanted each state to be represented in this group.

Delegates from states that had small populations, like Delaware, wanted all states to have the same number of members. "Unfair!" said states like Virginia that had large populations. "States with more people need more representatives."

In the end, the delegates decided to **compromise.** This means each side gives in a little to reach an agreement. The result was the Congress we have today. It has two parts, each called a house. In one house, the Senate, each state has two members. The other house is called the House of Representatives. Here each state has a different number of representatives, depending on the number of people in the state.

 **Which house did small states find fair? Which house did big states find fair?**

_____

**How many members did the first Senate have?**

_____

# The Federal System

Should the national government or the states be more powerful? The delegates also compromised on this question. The delegates shared the power between the states and the national, or federal, government. This sharing of power is called a **federal system.**

The federal government defends our country and mints the money. It also deals with other nations. The states make laws that take care of the daily life of Americans. For example, they control state school systems and state highways.

The delegates also divided the federal government into three parts, or branches. These are the legislative, executive, and judicial branches. These branches share the power of government. The legislative branch is Congress. The executive branch includes the President and many assistants. The judicial branch is made up of the Supreme Court and lower courts.

Look at the chart on this page. What is the first job of the legislative branch?

| Legislative Branch (Congress) | Executive Branch (President) | Judicial Branch (Courts) |
|---|---|---|
|  |  |  |
| **Senate** **House of Representatives** Makes the federal laws. Sets federal taxes. Approves appointments by President. May impeach the President. | **Executive Departments** Sees that federal laws are carried out. Approves or vetoes federal laws. Appoints ambassadors, judges, and other federal officials. Commands the armed forces. | **The Supreme Court of the United States** **Lower Courts** Decides what laws mean. Punishes lawbreakers. May rule that a law passed by Congress is unconstitutional (not in keeping with the Constitution). |

None of the three branches of the federal government can work alone. For example, only Congress can make laws. But the President must approve the laws by signing them. And the Supreme Court can decide whether the law goes against the Constitution.

The delegates made sure to create a system of **checks and balances.** This means that each branch checks, or limits, the power of the others. The power is then balanced among all three branches.

George Washington (top) was the first President of the United States. John Adams (bottom) was the second President.

**What does a system of checks and balances do for the three branches of government?**

## The Bill of Rights

After the delegates signed the Constitution, it did not become law right away. Before it could become law, two thirds of the states had to approve it. How many states did that make?

Several states said they would approve the Constitution, but only on one condition. They said it had to have a **bill of rights.** By this they meant a list of rights that every American should have. With the promise of a bill of rights, all 13 states approved the Constitution by 1790. George Washington said this was a victory "for all mankind."

The writers of the Constitution had made a way to change it, too. Changes to the Constitution are called **amendments.** In 1791, the first ten amendments to the Constitution were added. They are known as the Bill of Rights. These ten amendments explain the basic freedoms that all Americans have. These amendments also list the rights of all Americans.

What do you think the family living when the Constitution was written would have thought of the Bill of Rights? Write a journal entry about your family members' opinions of the Bill of Rights.

# The Bill of Rights

## What It Says

| | |
|---|---|
| Amendment 1 | **Basic freedoms.** Protects freedom of religion, freedom of speech, freedom of the press, freedom to hold meetings, and freedom to ask the government to correct problems. Keeps the government from creating an official religion. |
| Amendment 2 | **Right to bear arms.** Gives people the right to bear arms, subject to laws of state and federal governments. |
| Amendment 3 | **Quartering of soldiers.** Protects people from having to give room and board to soldiers. |
| Amendment 4 | **Freedom from unlawful searches and arrests.** Keeps the police from being able to search and arrest people unlawfully. |
| Amendment 5 | **Rights of people accused of crimes.** Protects people accused of crimes from being taken to trial unfairly and being given unfair punishments. |
| Amendment 6 | **Trial by jury.** Gives people accused of crimes the right to a speedy public trial by jury. Spells out how trial is to be conducted. |
| Amendment 7 | **Civil trials.** Gives people involved in lawsuits the right to a jury trial. |
| Amendment 8 | **Bails, fines, and punishments.** Protects people from unfair bails, fines, and punishments. |
| Amendment 9 | **Rights to the people.** People have more than just those rights listed in the Constitution. |
| Amendment 10 | **Rights reserved for the states and the people.** All powers not given to the federal government belong to the states or the people themselves. |

George Washington arrives at New York City to become the first President of the United States.

## Our Government Begins

George Washington became the country's first President in 1789. He served two four-year terms. He had been a popular general in the army. Now he became a popular President.

As President, Washington had to choose people to work in the new government. He had to find ways to pay for everything that was needed during the Revolution. He also had to find ways to get along with other countries. Courts had to be started. The country and the world were watching to see how the new government worked.

At first, the President ran the country from New York City. Then, between 1790 and 1800, our capital was Philadelphia. In 1800, the capital was moved again. The new location was Washington, D.C. This is still the capital of the United States today.

John Adams was Vice President with Washington. He became our second President. He was the first President to live in the new capital. He was also the first President to live in the new White House.

**Where was the first capital of the United States?**

# The French Revolution

The poor were tired of being hungry while the rich ate well. They were tired of paying many taxes while the rich paid no taxes. The poor were angry that a king could send them to prison with no trial. Only the rich were given good jobs. The poor decided to fight for their rights!

Were these American colonists? No, they were the people of France. But they were angry about the same kinds of unfairness. They heard of the Americans' successful fight for rights and freedom. They, too, wanted to fight for their rights.

On July 14, 1789, a mob of French men and women shouted "To the Bastille!" They attacked the Bastille, which was both a prison and a storehouse for weapons. The French Revolution had begun. It lasted for ten years, but finally the people of France won their rights.

**How was the French Revolution like the American Revolution?**

_____

_____

The French Revolution began with an attack on this prison.

# CHAPTER ✓ CHECKUP

**Complete each sentence. Circle the letter in front of the correct answer.**

1. Under the Articles of Confederation, the states had

   **a.** a strong federal government.
   **b.** a weak federal government.
   **c.** a judicial branch.
   **d.** federal taxes.

2. The basic law of the United States is the

   **a.** Constitution.
   **b.** system of checks and balances.
   **c.** President.
   **d.** federal system.

3. When people compromise, they

   **a.** give in a little to reach an agreement.
   **b.** refuse to change their ideas.
   **c.** promise not to change their minds.
   **d.** ask for more representatives.

4. The two houses of Congress are the House of Representatives and the

   **a.** Legislature.
   **b.** Senate.
   **c.** Capitol.
   **d.** Constitution.

5. The executive branch includes

   **a.** Congress.
   **b.** the courts.
   **c.** the President.
   **d.** the Constitution.

6. The part of the Constitution that explains the basic freedoms of Americans is

   **a.** the Articles of Confederation.
   **b.** the federal system.
   **c.** the Bill of Rights.
   **d.** the executive branch.

**THINKING AND WRITING**  Why does our government have a system of checks and balances?

_____

_____

_____

_____

_____

_____

_____

# A Growing Nation, 1800–1840

In 1800, the United States stretched north to Canada and south to Florida. It stretched from the Atlantic Ocean to the Mississippi River. In this chapter, you'll learn how the United States gained more land. And you'll see how this additional land more than doubled the size of our country.

## The Louisiana Purchase

Thomas Jefferson

Thomas Jefferson became the third President of the United States in 1801. One of Jefferson's hopes was to control the port of New Orleans. This city was in Louisiana. Louisiana was a colony owned by France. New Orleans was at the mouth of the Mississippi River. It was an important port city. American farmers sent their crops down the Mississippi to New Orleans. From there, crops were carried to large cities in the East. Jefferson wanted the United States to control this important port.

Jefferson offered France $10 million for the port. Would the French accept? The French amazed the Americans. In 1803, they sold New Orleans and the rest of Louisiana for only $15 million! This bargain is called the Louisiana Purchase.

Napoleon

The French leader Napoleon sold the land because he needed money to fight a war with Great Britain. Also, since no one had explored the territory, Napoleon thought it was worthless.

Jefferson also knew little about the land he had bought. Was it good farmland? How did the American Indians there feel about settlers? No one even knew how large the territory was! Jefferson decided to send explorers to Louisiana to find out.

 **Why did Jefferson want control of New Orleans?**

_____

## An Amazing Journey

Meriwether Lewis and William Clark led a group of 40 men who explored the land of the Louisiana Purchase. They started in St. Louis, Missouri, in the spring of 1804. They traveled by canoe along the Missouri River. They saw huge herds of buffalo. They met many groups of American Indians.

The explorers spent the winter in what is now North Dakota. They built a fort near a group of American Indians. There they met a French fur trapper and his wife, Sacajawea.

Sacajawea was a Shoshone from far to the west. She offered to lead the explorers across the Rocky Mountains.

During the trip, Lewis wrote in his diary about Sacajawea's help: "Our journey would have ended in failure without her aid."

 Look at the map on this page. Underline the starting point of Lewis and Clark's trip. Circle the names of the rivers they followed.

In what direction did Lewis and Clark travel?

_____

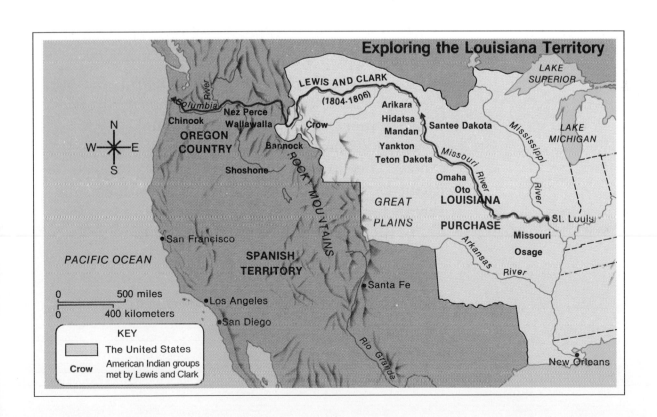

Sacajawea led Lewis and Clark to the Pacific Ocean.

Lewis and Clark finally reached the source, or beginning, of the Missouri River. They could see the snowy peaks of the Rocky Mountains. Now they needed horses to cross the mountains. Would the nearby Shoshone sell them horses?

The explorers made friends with all the American Indians they met along the way. But the Shoshone were angry. They thought that the explorers would upset their way of life. The chiefs who met Lewis and Clark wore war paint. The explorers were in terrible danger.

Then the head chief recognized the Shoshone guide. Sacajawea was his sister!

Now the Shoshone were happy to help Lewis and Clark. The Shoshone sold horses to the explorers. They led them over the Rocky Mountains.

Then the Shoshone helped the explorers build canoes. They canoed down the Columbia River to the Pacific Ocean. Where the Columbia River meets the Pacific, Lewis and Clark built a fort. They spent the winter there before returning to St. Louis in September 1806.

**Why weren't the Shoshone friendly at first?**

This painting shows one battle during the War of 1812.

## The War of 1812

When James Madison became President in 1808, he had a serious problem. Great Britain and France were at war. Each country told the United States not to trade with the other.

The French seized American ships to keep them from trading with Great Britain. The British captured American ships to keep them from trading with the French. The British also went on American ships. They took American sailors and made them work on British ships.

One group of American congressmen became very angry about what the British were doing. Most of them were from the southern and western states. They demanded that President James Madison declare war on Great Britain. They became known as the "War Hawks."

But in New England many people did not want to go to war with Great Britain. Much of the United States' shipping trade was based in New England. New Englanders feared that a war with Great Britain would destroy American shipping trade. In 1812 Congress, led by the "War Hawks," declared war on Great Britain.

**Why were many people in New England against going to war with Great Britain?**

Dolley Madison was the wife of President James Madison. Besides being very brave, Mrs. Madison was well known for her charm.

Great Britain had the most powerful navy in the world. But the small United States Navy was able to win several sea battles. The British Navy placed some warships all along the east coast of the United States. This is called a naval **blockade.** This meant that American ships could not take goods across the Atlantic Ocean. And goods on ships from other countries could not get into American harbors. Many American businesses lost money because of the blockade.

On land, the British beat the Americans in Washington, D.C. In 1814, they attacked and burned the White House. Dolley Madison, the wife of the President, acted very bravely. She escaped from the White House with important papers. She also saved a painting of George Washington.

After they left Washington, D.C., the British Navy sailed for Baltimore, Maryland. There, Fort McHenry guarded the harbor. The British fired on the fort all day. Firing continued during the night of September 13, 1814.

**What brave thing did Dolley Madison do?**

## "The Flag Was Still There"

A young American, Francis Scott Key, watched that battle on the night of September 13, 1814. At dawn he saw the American flag still flying over the fort. The Americans still controlled the fort! Key wrote a poem, "The Star-Spangled Banner," about what he had seen. It became our national **anthem,** or song.

The British and the Americans signed a peace treaty in Ghent, Belgium, on December 24, 1814. The treaty ended the war. But another battle, the Battle of New Orleans, was fought on January 8, 1815, before news of the treaty reached the United States.

The War of 1812 was an unusual war. The treaty called for everything to go back to the same way it had been before the war! The United States gained no new territory, and neither did the British. But one result of the war was that the United States became more sure of itself as a nation. It had been able to hold its own in war against the powerful nation of Great Britain.

**Why do you think it took so long for news of the treaty to reach the United States?**

_____

_____

Francis Scott Key saw the American flag still flying over Fort McHenry.

## "Old Hickory"

In 1828, Andrew Jackson was elected the seventh President of the United States. For the first time, a person from the frontier was President.

Jackson had been one of the first lawyers on the Tennessee frontier. He had also been elected to Congress from Tennessee. And his victory at the Battle of New Orleans made him an American hero.

His frontier neighbors liked Jackson. They liked the idea that a frontiersman could become a success in government. Jackson became famous all over the West. People called him "Old Hickory." Hickory is the strongest and toughest tree in the forests of Tennessee.

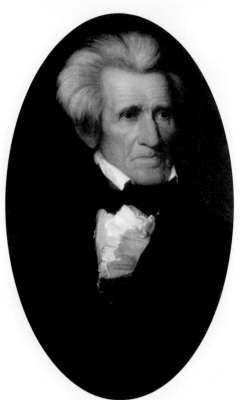

Andrew Jackson

## The Age of the Common Man

Ideas about voting were changing in America. In the first 13 states, not everyone was allowed to vote. Only white men who owned land could vote. Women, African Americans, American Indians, and poor white men could not vote.

In the new western states, all white men could vote. In this way, the frontier states were more **democratic.** *Democratic* means "treating people as equals." It means "having respect for ordinary people."

By 1828, most of the older states also allowed all white men to vote. This change in voting rights was an important step. It was a step toward democracy. For this reason, Andrew Jackson's time is called the Age of the **Common** Man. Here, *common* means "ordinary."

**How were the frontier states different from the first 13 states?**

_____

_____

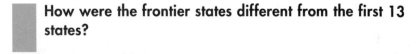
Suppose it is the year 1828. Time has passed since your last journal entries. Your family decides to move to one of the frontier states. What would it be like to be a new frontier settler? Write some journal entries about life on the frontier. Remember that your character has gotten older.

# The Trail of Tears

The United States slowly spread westward. There was often trouble between settlers and American Indians. Many treaties were signed between the government and different American Indian groups. The treaties promised that the settlers would take only a certain amount of land.

But again and again the treaties were broken and fighting began. Sometimes the settlers started fighting because they wanted more land. Sometimes the American Indians didn't accept the treaties. They fought to save the land their ancestors had lived on for hundreds of years.

The Cherokee of Georgia and Alabama lived on land they received in a treaty. Then settlers found gold on Cherokee land. The settlers wanted the Cherokee to move. The government was on the side of the settlers. The Cherokee were forced off their land.

During the winter of 1839, Cherokee men, women, and children had to walk to Oklahoma. It was very cold. There wasn't enough food. About one out of four Cherokee people died on the way. This terrible march is called the Trail of Tears.

**What does the name Trail of Tears tell you about how the American Indians felt?**

_____

The trip to Oklahoma was long and hard for the Cherokee.

Ben Nighthorse Campbell

*Mississippi, Erie, Miami, Alaska,* and *Illinois*—these names show where American Indians once lived. Many American towns, rivers, and states still have American Indian names.

Today, about half of all American Indians live in the western United States. Some live on **reservations.** These are special lands that have been set aside for American Indians. Children on reservations go to school. Grown-ups do many jobs. Some work on ranches, on farms, in stores, or in oil fields. Some people make jewelry or weave rugs like their ancestors have done for hundreds of years. These activities help their American Indian culture survive.

More than half of the American Indians in the United States do not live on reservations. American Indians are United States citizens and can vote, buy land, and hold government office. Ben Nighthorse Campbell is a member of the Cheyenne group of American Indians. He was a senator for Colorado from 1992 to 2004. He was a representative before that.

 **Why do you think it is important to learn an art such as rug weaving?**

_____

_____

This Navajo girl learns from her grandmother how to weave rugs.

# CHAPTER ✓ CHECKUP

**Complete each sentence. Circle the letter in front of the correct answer.**

1. As President, Jefferson hoped to
   a. move the nation's capital to New York.
   b. win a war with Spain.
   c. control the port of New Orleans.
   d. travel throughout Europe.

2. The Louisiana Purchase added land to the United States that was
   a. east of the Mississippi River.
   b. north of Lake Michigan.
   c. north of the Columbia River.
   d. west of the Mississippi River.

3. Napoleon surprised President Jefferson by
   a. fighting a war with Great Britain.
   b. selling the Louisiana Territory.
   c. closing the port of New Orleans.
   d. exploring the Louisiana Territory.

4. Lewis and Clark are famous because they
   a. explored the land of the Louisiana Purchase.
   b. built a fort near the Pacific Ocean.
   c. canoed the Missouri River.
   d. met Sacajawea.

5. When the British took sailors off American ships, this led to
   a. the War of 1812.
   b. trade with Great Britain.
   c. war with France.
   d. the capture of British ships.

6. During Andrew Jackson's time, an important step toward democracy was
   a. allowing everyone who owned land to vote.
   b. allowing all people to vote.
   c. allowing anyone from the first 13 states to vote.
   d. allowing all white men to vote.

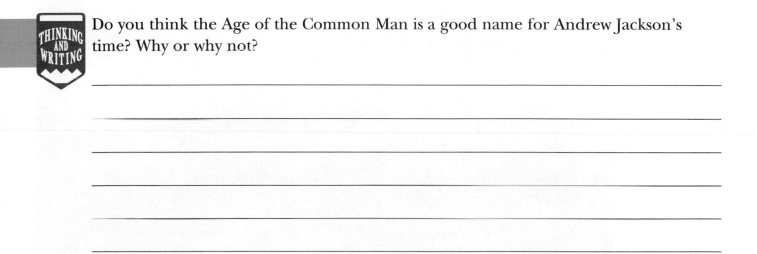

**THINKING AND WRITING** Do you think the Age of the Common Man is a good name for Andrew Jackson's time? Why or why not?

_____

_____

_____

_____

_____

_____

# Westward Expansion, 1830–1850

In 1800, Kentucky was called the West. It was west of the first 13 states. Later, the West was California. This chapter tells how the United States grew west across an entire continent.

Many people left their homes and farms in the East to go west. They headed for the frontier. They wanted land, adventure, and the chance to start a new life. We call these frontier settlers **pioneers.**

## Pioneer Life

The trip west wasn't easy. Some pioneers traveled by wagon. Oxen pulled the heavy wagons.

Other pioneers traveled by water. But river travel could be dangerous. Rivers often flooded in the spring. Sometimes boats turned over.

 **Why do you think wagons were a good way to travel?**

_____

_____

This pioneer family's oxen had trouble in the desert because there wasn't enough food or water.

Once the settlers reached their new home in Kentucky, what did they see? Forest! Each family's first job was to cut down trees. They cleared the land and plowed it. Then they planted crops.

Next, they built a house. Most pioneers lived in a one-room log cabin. Thick mud patched the cracks between the logs.

Families were on their own much of the time. They made all their own clothing, tools, and furniture. For food, they planted crops and raised animals. They hunted and fished.

Pioneer families also helped their neighbors. Neighbors helped each other build houses and barns. Together they harvested crops.

They tried to make everyday jobs more pleasant by turning them into a party. At a quilting bee, for example, people combined work and fun. Women told stories and sang songs while they sewed. Helping out was also part of pioneer life.

**Look at the picture below. What are two ways the pioneers got food?**

_____

_____

(above) People of all ages help at this quilting bee. (below) A father and his friend come home after a good hunting trip.

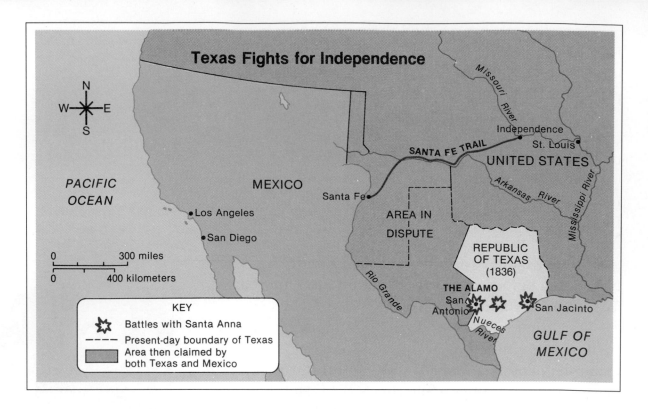

Texas Fights for Independence

## New Trade Routes

Traders as well as pioneers helped open up the West. In 1821, Mexico won its independence from Spain. Spain had not let Mexicans trade with Americans. But now Mexico wanted American trade.

One big trading center was the Mexican city of Santa Fe. It was a place of beautiful houses and churches. Americans traded cloth and tools for furs and Mexican silver in Santa Fe. To get there, traders followed the Santa Fe Trail.

The Mexican government owned the land that is now Texas. The Mexicans wanted the land to be settled. So they invited Americans to live there. Soon 20,000 Americans had settled in Texas. They built farms and cattle ranches.

At first, things went well. Then the Americans decided they didn't want to be governed by Mexico. They wanted to govern themselves. They decided to break away from Mexico. But this decision made the Mexicans angry. Texas belonged to Mexico.

 **Look at the map on this page. Where does the Santa Fe Trail begin?**

## Texas Independence

In 1836, a Mexican general named Santa Anna led an army of about 6,000 men into Texas. They marched toward the town of San Antonio. There, about 200 Americans protected the town in a fort called the Alamo.

The Mexican Army surrounded the Alamo. For two weeks, the Americans fought off the Mexican Army. On March 6, 1836, Santa Anna and his men climbed the walls of the fort. At the end of the day, all the American soldiers in the Alamo had been killed.

But a month later, the Texans won an important fight. A man named Sam Houston led a surprise attack against Santa Anna. As he led the attack, he yelled "Remember the Alamo!" Santa Anna was captured. He agreed that Texas could become an independent country.

Sam Houston was the first president of Texas. Texas became known as the Lone Star Republic. This was because it was part of neither Mexico nor the United States. In 1845, Texas joined the United States. Now it was the Lone Star State.

 Look at the map on page 88. Circle the name of the battle at San Antonio. Who won the battle there?

_____

Americans held the Alamo for nearly two weeks against the Mexican Army.

A settler painted this view of his Texas farm.

## War with Mexico

In 1846, the United States and Mexico went to war. Many Americans wanted Mexican lands. And Mexico was angry because Texas had become a state.

The war lasted two years. In the end, the United States won. Mexico agreed to give the United States huge pieces of land. The United States got part of what is today Arizona, New Mexico, Colorado, and Wyoming. It also got all of California, Nevada, and Utah. The United States now stretched "from sea to shining sea."

**How did the United States get California?**

## California, Here I Come!

Mexico and the United States didn't know that there was gold in California. In January 1848, gold was discovered in mountain streams in California. Thousands of people rushed into the hills and mountains of California looking for gold. The Gold Rush had begun!

By 1849, the rest of the world had heard about the gold. Thousands more people rushed to California in search of gold. The people who went to California to look for gold were called **forty-niners.** Before the Gold Rush, California had a population of 15,000. In 1849, there were over 50,000 people!

Small towns in California grew to big cities. San Francisco, for example, had a population of only 800 before the Gold Rush. It soon had a population of about 35,000.

People found out that mining was hard work. It wasn't easy to become rich by mining for gold. Most miners had only simple tools, so mining was hard work.

 **What kinds of things would the forty-niners need besides tools?**

A lot of miners used a process called placer mining. They poured water over boxes full of dirt, sand, and gravel. They hoped the mixture also contained flakes and nuggets of gold. Gold is heavier than sand or gravel. The gold would sink to the bottom of the boxes, and the sand and gravel would be washed out.

Most miners did not find much gold. Some people gave up mining and opened stores. They made money selling miners what they needed. There were other problems, too. There were no police to keep order. Some people took the law into their own hands.

How could California solve its law and order problems? One answer was to become a state. The people elected a legislature and wrote a constitution. Then California asked to join the United States.

Miners look for gold in California.

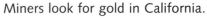

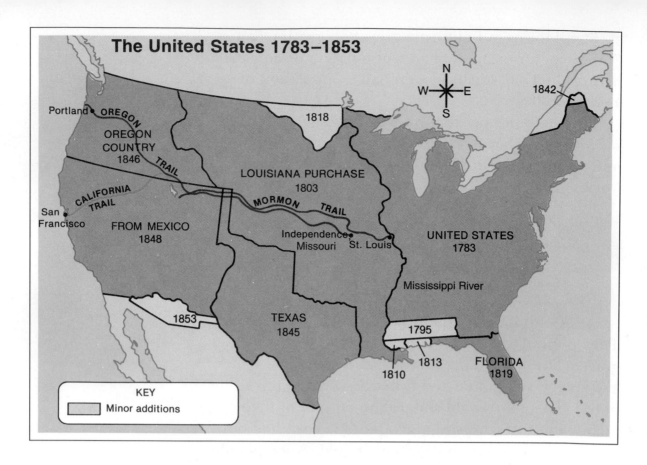

**The United States 1783–1853**

Portland • OREGON
OREGON COUNTRY 1846
CALIFORNIA TRAIL
San Francisco •
FROM MEXICO 1848
1853
1818
LOUISIANA PURCHASE 1803
MORMON TRAIL
Independence Missouri •
St. Louis •
UNITED STATES 1783
Mississippi River
TEXAS 1845
1795
1810
1813
FLORIDA 1819
1842

KEY
Minor additions

## How the United States Grew

The map on this page shows when different areas became part of the United States. The map also shows the trails that led the pioneers west.

Remember that Lewis and Clark explored the territory of the Louisiana Purchase in the early 1800s. Other explorers traveling west from the Mississippi River first found the flat grassy plains that stretch for hundreds of miles in all directions. There were few trees on these plains.

Beyond the plains, explorers had to cross the Rocky Mountains. Some of the explorers made maps of the easiest way to cross the Rocky Mountains and the desert areas west of the Rocky Mountains. Eventually explorers got all the way to the California coast.

Some of the explorers helped set up trade routes like the Santa Fe Trail. They also set up other routes west. One of these routes was the Oregon Trail, which led to Oregon Country.

 **Find the Oregon Trail on the map. Where does the Oregon Trail begin?**

It was hard for pioneers to cross the rugged Rocky Mountains to reach Oregon.

People back east began to hear about the good farmland in Oregon Country. They wanted to move there. In 1843, the first large group of pioneers set out in covered wagons. They followed the Oregon Trail. It was a very hard trip. Imagine crossing the Rocky Mountains in a covered wagon! Sometimes the pioneers didn't have enough food or water. The trip to Oregon took about six months.

The Oregon Country was claimed by both Great Britain and the United States. Settlers from both Great Britain and the United States went to Oregon, but most of the settlers were Americans. Great Britain finally gave up its claim to the Oregon Country, and it officially became part of the United States.

 **Look at the map on page 92. In what year did the Oregon Country become part of the United States?**

---

**Find another trail that leads west. Trace the route west.**

Suppose it's the year 1850. You are the grandson or granddaughter of one of the people who started a journal in 1783. Your family decides once again to pack up and go west. Choose one of the trails shown on the map and find out what a journey on that trail was like. Write an entry for your family's journal about the trip west.

# Estevan Ochoa

Estevan Ochoa

Estevan Ochoa was one of the people who helped Tucson, Arizona, become the city it is today.

Before the middle of the 1800s, the area that is today Arizona was part of Mexico. There were no railroads in the area. People used mules to haul goods from place to place. This business was called freighting.

As a little boy, Estevan Ochoa rode with his father's trading mules all over northern Mexico, the Southwest, and along the Santa Fe Trail to Independence, Missouri.

When Estevan grew up, he formed his own freighting business. He used mules to pull large wagon trains loaded with goods. He helped change Tucson, Arizona, from a small frontier town into a bustling trade community. By 1865, freighting was the most important business in Arizona. Ochoa and his partner supplied Tucson with goods they needed, like harnesses and wagons. They also supplied ranches that were far from town.

Ochoa's business was very successful. He was a good businessman. Part of his success had to do with the kind of community Tucson was. In Tucson, Mexican Americans held many important positions in the town. They started schools. Ochoa helped start Arizona's public school system. He believed that people needed a good education to succeed. In 1875, the people of Tucson elected Ochoa mayor.

When railroads reached Tucson in the late 1800s, Ochoa's freighting business suffered. The railroads were much faster than Ochoa's mules. Ochoa died not long after the railroads ended the need for mule trains. At his funeral, the people of Tucson honored him for his many achievements within the community.

**How did Estevan Ochoa help the children of Arizona?**

# CHAPTER ✓ CHECKUP

**Complete each sentence. Circle the letter in front of the correct answer.**

1. Pioneers were people who
   a. settled the frontier.
   b. stayed in their homes in the East.
   c. attended quilting bees.
   d. were afraid of adventure.

2. One important trading route to Mexico was
   a. the route taken by Lewis and Clark.
   b. the Oregon Trail.
   c. the Mormon Trail.
   d. the Santa Fe Trail.

3. Americans in Texas wanted to break away from Mexico because they
   a. needed more water for crops.
   b. wanted to move north again.
   c. didn't like Mexican laws.
   d. changed from farming to ranching.

4. Sam Houston was
   a. a Mexican general.
   b. the president of Texas.
   c. a school teacher.
   d. a trader living in Santa Fe.

5. After a war, Mexico had to give the United States land that included
   a. Florida and Louisiana.
   b. Kentucky and North Carolina.
   c. California and Nevada.
   d. Texas only.

6. The Gold Rush was
   a. the rush to find gold in California.
   b. a mining tool.
   c. another name for the forty-niners.
   d. a mining town.

**THINKING AND WRITING**

What are some things we could use on a trip today that the pioneers had to do without?

_____

_____

_____

_____

_____

_____

_____

# Reading a Historical Route Map

In the 1800s, the Cherokee and other American Indian groups including the Choctaw, Chickasaw, and Seminole were forced to move to reservations. The map below shows where the groups lived before they had to move. It also shows the routes they took to reservations in Indian Territory.

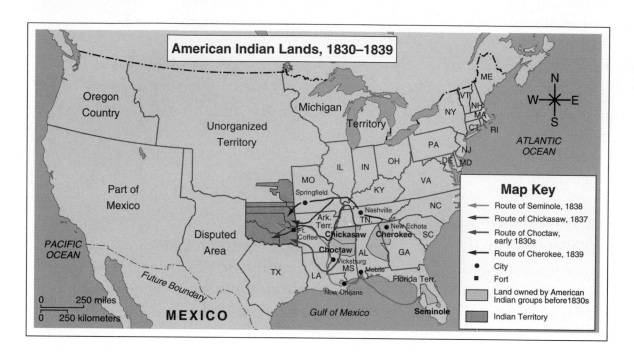

**American Indian Lands, 1830–1839**

Map Key
- Route of Seminole, 1838
- Route of Chickasaw, 1837
- Route of Choctaw, early 1830s
- Route of Cherokee, 1839
- City
- Fort
- Land owned by American Indian groups before1830s
- Indian Territory

1. Look at the map key. The American Indians marched to what is now Oklahoma. What was the name of that area?

   _____

2. In what year were the Chickasaw forced to leave their land?

   _____

3. Did the Choctaw have more land before or after they moved to the reservation in Indian Territory?

   _____

4. Which American Indian group had to travel farthest from their original land?

   _____

5. Shade the area of the map that was part of Mexico.

Now it's time to finish your unit project. Think about all the things that happened in our country between 1783 and 1853. Talk with your team to answer questions like these.

- **Why were the Bill of Rights and the Constitution important?**

- **What was life like on the frontier?**

- **What problems did the pioneers face on the Oregon Trail and other trails?**

Decide how you want to present your team's family journals. Choose one of these ideas or use one of your own ideas.

➤ Arrange the journal entries your team wrote in an album. Add illustrations of important events. You could also include pictures of tools, clothing, and other items used by pioneers.

➤ Have each member of your team take the role of one of the family members. Work together to describe or act out for the class a part of the family's history.

# UNIT 4

# A Divided Nation

During the time the West was opening up, things were changing in the East, too. In the North, factories opened and cities grew bigger. In the South, more and more people made money growing cotton. They also used more and more slaves to plant and harvest the cotton. The North and the South were growing in different directions. Finally, their differences caused a conflict called the Civil War.

In this unit you will learn the answers to questions like these.

- What caused the Civil War?
- What part did Abraham Lincoln play in history?
- Which side won the war?

## UNIT PROJECT

Start a team project. Learn about inventions of the 1800s. How did they change life for Americans? Work on your project as you read Unit 4.

# The North and the South, 1820–1860

In this chapter, you will read about different ways of life in the North and the South. The South was a land of plantations and farms. In the North were factories, growing cities, and railroads.

## Factories

Starting in the 1700s, people invented machines that were run by water or steam power. These machines could make goods quickly and cheaply. Before machines, goods such as cloth were made by hand in small shops and at home. Because products made by machines were cheaper, more people were able to buy them.

But only rich people could buy machines because they cost a lot. These people hired workers to run the machines in factories. They paid the workers from the money made by selling the products. A few workers using machines could make as much cloth as many workers doing it by hand.

In the North, water from streams powered the machines. Coal from northern mines could be burned to make steam for power. Business people there started factories to make products.

Workers in this cotton textile mill operate large looms that greatly increased fabric production in the 1800s.

**How did people produce the goods they needed before machines were invented?**

_____

_____

_____

# The Railroad Boom

Between 1830 and 1850, there was a railroad boom. Dozens of railroads were built between towns and cities. Most of them were in the Northeast.

Many railroads were built by business people in the cities. They wanted an easy way to bring **raw materials** to their factories. Raw materials are what factory products, like cloth and tools, are made of. Wool, cotton, and iron are raw materials. Business people also needed to ship the finished products to buyers. Trains brought factory products from the East to the West. They brought farm products from the West to the East. Railroads meant that travel was faster and cheaper.

 **Look at the picture on this page. You can see two different ways of moving things. What are they?**

_____

_____

This is a painting of a railroad yard in Massachusetts.

The railroad brought factory products to more people. So more and more factories were built. Factories meant jobs. Many people left their farms to work in the factories. Some people couldn't support themselves on their small farms. Others hoped for a better life in cities.

But factory life was hard. Factories were often dark, dirty, and unsafe. The pay was low. The hours were long. Sometimes even children had to work 14 hours a day.

## The Growth of Cities

As more people moved to find work, small factory towns grew into cities. New buildings went up. Streets were paved. Shops opened to sell clothes and food to busy factory workers.

Cities were very busy places. They had eating places, hotels, and theaters. There were books, magazines, and newspapers. People could always find something to see or do.

 **Why did people go to work in factories?**

_____

_____

(above) A young girl works in a New England factory. (below) The streets of New York City were busy even in the 1830s.

(above) The harvest was a busy time on a cotton plantation. (below) The cotton gin changed life in the South forever.

## When Cotton Was "King"

People were building railroads and factories in the North. Meanwhile, on plantations and farms in the South, people were growing crops for sale. They grew tobacco, rice, and corn.

Southern plantations also grew cotton. But cotton has small black seeds in it. It took long hours to remove the seeds by hand. So farmers couldn't make enough money on cotton.

Then a young man named Eli Whitney invented the cotton gin. This machine cleaned cotton much faster than people working by hand. In fact, it could clean as much cotton in one day as 50 people could!

Soon cotton was the most important crop in the South. Plantations shipped cotton to the North and to England. There, factories turned the cotton into cloth. Cotton growers got rich. Cotton was "king" in the South.

 **What made cotton the most important crop in the South? Why?**

 With your team, find out more about the cotton gin and how it worked.

Planting and picking cotton were still done by hand. So big cotton plantations needed more workers. Slaves had worked on plantations for a long time. Now plantation owners said they needed more slaves to grow more cotton.

## Slave Life

What was life like for slaves on Southern plantations? Slaves were not free. They could not choose where to live or how to make a living. Slaves could be bought and sold. Their families could be separated.

Most slaves worked in the fields. They spent their days plowing fields, planting seeds, or picking cotton. Other slaves did household work in the owner's home. They took care of the owner's children. They cooked and served food. Slaves were not paid for any of the jobs they did. When slaves were too sick to work, they were punished.

Few slaves could read or write. The owners felt that learning might give slaves too many ideas. Also, schooling would take time away from work.

**How did slaves make money for their owners?**

_____

(above) When slaves were sold, families were often broken apart. (below) Photography was invented in the 1800s. This is a photograph of slaves working.

# The Missouri Compromise

By 1820, there were 22 states in the United States. Eleven states allowed slavery. They were called **slave states.** Eleven states did not allow slavery. They were called **free states.**

Then Missouri asked to become a state. Would Missouri become a slave state or a free state? Northerners and Southerners fought about this in Congress. Both groups had the same number of senators. Both groups wanted Missouri's senators on their side.

Congress finally decided that Missouri should become a slave state. The next state, Maine, should be a free state. This agreement is known as the Missouri Compromise. People hoped the Missouri Compromise would solve the problem of slavery in the new states.

 **After the Missouri Compromise, how many slave states and free states were there?**

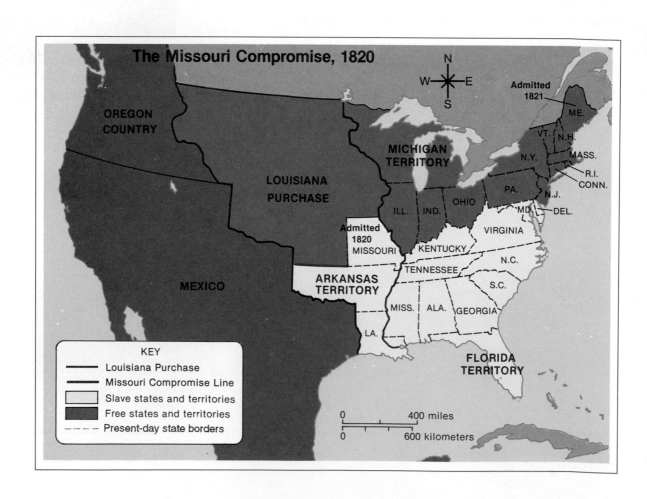

The Missouri Compromise, 1820

OREGON COUNTRY

LOUISIANA PURCHASE

MEXICO

ARKANSAS TERRITORY

MICHIGAN TERRITORY

Admitted 1820 MISSOURI

ILL. IND. OHIO

KENTUCKY

TENNESSEE

MISS. ALA. GEORGIA

LA.

VIRGINIA

N.C.

S.C.

FLORIDA TERRITORY

Admitted 1821

ME.

VT. N.H.

N.Y. MASS.

R.I. CONN.

PA.

N.J.

MD. DEL.

**KEY**
— Louisiana Purchase
— Missouri Compromise Line
☐ Slave states and territories
■ Free states and territories
- - - Present-day state borders

0    400 miles
0    600 kilometers

## Escape from Slavery

Some men and women were able to escape from slavery. Frederick Douglass was one slave who escaped. He escaped in 1838 and went north. In the North, he wrote and spoke against slavery.

In his talks, Douglass said, "I appear before you this evening as a thief and a robber." Then he added "I stole this head, these limbs, this body from my master, and ran off with them."

Douglass suggested setting up a way for slaves to escape to the North. His plan was called the Underground Railroad. But it wasn't really a railroad. The slaves were called "passengers." On their way north, they stopped at "stations." These were homes where they would be safe. "Conductors" were guides who helped slaves along the way. About 50,000 slaves escaped on the Underground Railroad.

(above) Frederick Douglass had a plan to help other slaves escape. (below) Harriet Tubman was an escaped slave who led many other slaves to freedom.

 **Was Frederick Douglass really a thief? What did he mean when he called himself one?**

_____

One of the conductors on the Underground Railroad was Harriet Tubman. Tubman had been born a slave. But she escaped and led other slaves to freedom. She made 19 trips to the North. She led more than 300 slaves to freedom.

Tubman and other helpers on the Underground Railroad were very brave. Their work was very dangerous. Congress said it was against the law to help runaway slaves. Slave owners offered a $40,000 reward for Harriet Tubman's capture.

 **How did Harriet Tubman fight against slavery?**

_____

Another woman helped fight slavery in another way. In 1851, Harriet Beecher Stowe wrote a book called _Uncle Tom's Cabin_. It was based on true stories. The book told about the hard life of some slaves in Kentucky. Millions of people read this book. It made them think about how wrong slavery was. In time, more and more people began to think that slavery should be ended.

## The Compromise of 1850

After the Missouri Compromise of 1820, the North and the South each had the same number of senators in Congress.

But slavery was still a problem that divided the nation. Many people in the North felt slavery should be ended. In the South, landowners were afraid that they could not grow cotton without slaves. They thought if cotton stopped being "king," everyone in the South would become poor.

By 1850, the United States had grown from 24 states to 30 states. There were 15 slave states and 15 free states. Then California wanted to become a free state. There were no new slave states. How would the North and the South compromise?

The Compromise of 1850 said that California would become a free state. It also made a new law. This law said that all runaway slaves had to be returned to their owners.

 **Which part of the Compromise of 1850 did the North like? Which part did the South like?**

Even as a young man, Abraham Lincoln was against slavery. Here he is shown splitting logs.

## Lincoln and Slavery

One Northerner who was against slavery was Abraham Lincoln. In 1858, he ran for senator from Illinois. Lincoln said that the United States couldn't have half free states and half slave states. He said, "A house divided against itself cannot stand." When Lincoln said "house," he meant "nation." Lincoln lost the election for senator. But now people knew who he was. They knew how he felt about slavery.

Two years later, in 1860, Lincoln ran for President. Some Southern states said they would leave the United States if Lincoln won. They were afraid they would have to give up slavery. They felt that the North and the South were enemies.

Lincoln won the election of 1860. What would the Southern states do now that Lincoln was President?

When Lincoln was elected President in 1860, Sojourner Truth was an old woman. She had been born a slave in 1797. Her real name was Isabella. She lived on a farm in New York State.

Sojourner was bought and sold several times. She married and had five children, all slaves. It made her sad and angry when two of her daughters were sold away from her. Finally she ran away. A year later, in 1828, slavery was outlawed in New York State. She went to New York City and worked as a servant.

But Sojourner wanted more. She wanted to speak out against injustice. She wanted to travel and spread God's word. She called herself Sojourner Truth. A sojourner is a traveler.

Sojourner set off on her travels with only 25 cents. She traveled all over the country. Sojourner became a well-known speaker. She spoke against slavery. She spoke for the rights of women. At that time, neither women nor African Americans could vote or own property.

Once, at a big meeting, Sojourner heard a man say that women weren't equal to men. Sojourner stood up and answered him. "I have labored, I have planted and harvested crops. And aren't I a woman?" This speech made her famous.

Sojourner also helped escaped slaves find homes and jobs in the North. She did what she could do to help African Americans have a better life.

She was invited to the White House by President Lincoln. When Sojourner died she was 86 years old. Her death made many people very sad.

Sojourner Truth was the most famous African American woman of her time.

**What two groups could not vote during Sojourner Truth's time?**

_____

_____

107

Southerners also thought that the United States government was becoming too strong. They did not think the government had the right to tell them how they should live. Southerners felt that if they stayed in the United States, the North would control them. So several Southern states decided they had no choice. They decided to **secede,** or leave, the United States.

## The Southern States Secede

By March 1861, seven Southern states had seceded. These seven states had formed a new nation—the Confederate States of America. Soon four more states joined. Would Lincoln do anything to get them back into the United States? The answer was yes.

The Northern states called themselves the Union. President Lincoln said the Southern states did not have the right to leave the Union. If necessary, he would fight to keep the nation united.

 **What was the capital of the Confederate States of America? Use the map below to find the answer.**

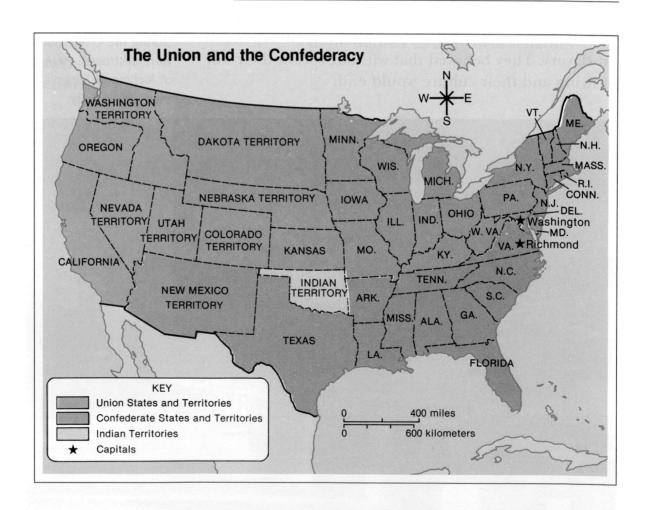

The Union and the Confederacy

KEY
Union States and Territories
Confederate States and Territories
Indian Territories
★ Capitals

## The Civil War Begins

There were Union forts on Confederate land, and the Southern states wanted to take over the forts. Charleston, South Carolina, wanted to take over Fort Sumter, which was in the city's harbor. The soldiers in the fort were almost out of food and water. Lincoln had to decide whether to try to send supplies or to give up the fort. He sent supplies.

Lincoln sent a message to the leaders of South Carolina. He told them, "I am sending our soldiers bread, not bullets." Now the South finally had to decide. Should the Confederate states let the supplies in or attack the fort and begin a war? On April 12, 1861, cannons from the city of Charleston fired on the fort. The war had begun.

(above) General Robert E. Lee led the Confederate Army. (below) General Thomas "Stonewall" Jackson was one of the Confederacy's best generals.

## The South Has Early Success— and Problems

Both the Union and the Confederate states thought the war would be short. Each thought the other side would give up after one or two **defeats,** or losses. But they were both wrong. The battle for Fort Sumter only lasted two days. But the war lasted four years.

**When did the Civil War start?**

**Where was the first battle fought?**

_____

Early in the war, the South won more battles. One reason for this was that the Southern generals, such as Robert E. Lee and Thomas "Stonewall" Jackson, were very good generals. They were better than the Northern generals they fought against.

111

These photographs show the regulation uniforms worn by soldiers during the Civil War. The Confederate soldiers (top) wore gray uniforms and the Union soldiers (bottom) wore blue uniforms.

In the First Battle of Bull Run in July 1861, "Stonewall" Jackson and other Confederate leaders showed how good they were. They crushed the Union **troops,** or soldiers. Now the Union knew that the war would not be short or easy to win.

But these early Southern victories hurt the South. These battles used up too much of what the South needed to win the war. The South, unlike the North, did not have as many men who could fight in the war. It did not have as many factories to make the guns, uniforms, and other supplies that were needed for the war. Sometimes Confederate troops marched barefoot because they could not get shoes.

The South could not get supplies from Europe because the North had placed warships all along the coastline of the South. Remember that this kind of strategy is called a blockade. With the blockade, the North sealed off the Southern ports. No ships could bring new supplies or help to the South.

The South did not lack food. It had enough farmland and people to raise crops. The problem was delivering the food to the people. The railroads in the South had been built to connect cotton plantation areas to port cities. The railroads did not link farms that produced food to places that needed food. Some Southerners almost starved because of the transportation problems.

During the war the South did build some new railroads, but most of the new railroad lines were built so soldiers could be moved from place to place.

**What were some problems the South had early in the Civil War?**

_____

_____

Find out more about some machines used during the Civil War. What goods did factories make to help soldiers during the war?

# Transportation in the South

The South had more transportation problems than the North did. Roads in the South were not as good as roads in the North. The South did not have as many lakes and canals that could be used for shipping. And most important, they did not have as good a railroad system as the North.

A double bar graph uses color and shape to show two kinds of information at one time. It tells you how two things are alike and different. Look at the double bar graph below. Compare the lengths of the bars. How many more miles of railroad track did the North have?

_____

Why were railroads important during the Civil War?

_____

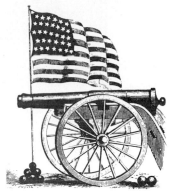

These were the flags that the Confederate states and the Union carried.

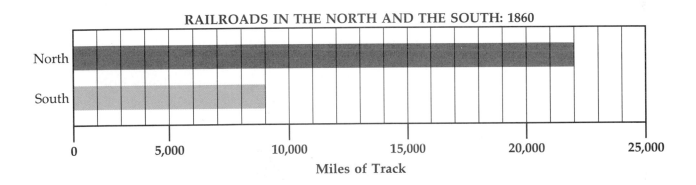

**RAILROADS IN THE NORTH AND THE SOUTH: 1860**

North

South

| 0 | 5,000 | 10,000 | 15,000 | 20,000 | 25,000 |

Miles of Track

Railroads were important in the war. They could carry many soldiers and supplies over long distances.

African American soldiers like these men fought bravely in the Union Army. Twenty-one of them won the nation's highest military award, the Medal of Honor.

## The Emancipation Proclamation

In September 1862, the Union Army defeated the South at the Battle of Antietam in Maryland. Thousands of soldiers were killed and wounded on both sides. But it was an important victory for the Union. Because of it, President Lincoln felt that he and the Union were strong enough for a bold decision.

So on January 1, 1863, the President signed the Emancipation Proclamation. This was an order that promised that Northern armies would free slaves in the Confederate states. President Lincoln wanted to win more support for the North.

The proclamation also ordered the use of African American troops in the Union Army. Many African Americans from the free states wanted to fight in the war. Most of them had been born in the North. But many were runaway slaves from the South.

 **Which Army did the Emancipation Proclamation allow African Americans to join?**

The African American soldiers fought bravely in the war. By the end of the war, over 180,000 African Americans had served in the fight for freedom.

## A War-Weary Land

The South had started the war with better generals than the North had. But President Lincoln found two generals who were as good as Lee and Jackson. Their names were Ulysses S. Grant and William T. Sherman. They soon were winning battles. But it took almost two years before the North began to win most of the battles.

On July 1, 1863, a three-day battle began at Gettysburg, Pennsylvania. Over 160,000 Union and Confederate soldiers fought there. By the end of the battle, General Lee's Confederate Army was very weak. The South was never able to fight a major battle after that.

The fighting continued for two more years, however. It was not until April 9, 1865, that General Lee surrendered to General Grant. The Civil War was finally over.

 **Look at the map on this page. Circle the names of the battles on the map. Were most of the major battles of the Civil War fought in the North or the South?**

_____

(top) General Ulysses S. Grant
(bottom) General William T. Sherman

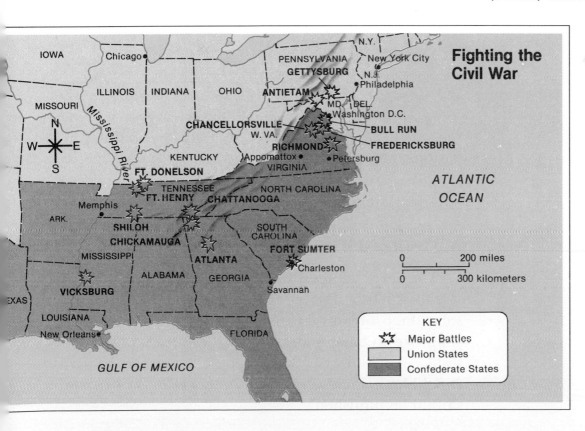

Fighting the Civil War

KEY
- Major Battles
- Union States
- Confederate States

(above) Richmond, Virginia, was in ruins by the end of the Civil War. (below) President Abraham Lincoln

## After the War

The Civil War kept the South from leaving the United States. It also put an end to slavery in our country. But thousands and thousands of Americans had been killed or wounded. Much of the South lay in ruins. Cities and towns were burned to the ground. Factories and farms were destroyed.

**What were two important results of the Civil War?**

_____

_____

President Lincoln said the nation was like a wounded soldier. It was time, he said, "to **bind up** the nation's wounds." Bind up means "to close." If the wounds were bound up, they would heal. If they were left open, the nation would not heal.

## A Troubled Time

The years between 1865 and 1877 are called Reconstruction. During this time the nation tried to solve the problems created by the Civil War. It was supposed to be a time of healing, but for a while, things just got worse. Some people felt that the South should be helped to recover. Others felt that the South should be punished.

President Abraham Lincoln did not live to see Reconstruction. Only five days after the war was over, Abraham Lincoln was shot and killed.

During Reconstruction, there were many problems in the South. Most people had to begin all over again. The war had left them with nothing. Congress sent the Army to the South. For a time, Northern generals governed the people there. Congress also passed a law that people could not vote or govern if they had been part of the Confederate government. These actions made Southerners angry.

**Why did Congress send the Army to the South?**

_____

## Free But Not Equal

There were many problems for African Americans following the war. Southerners made laws called Black Codes. Their purpose was to keep African Americans from having the same freedoms as other people.

Life was hard for most African Americans after the Civil War. This large family lived in a one-room cabin.

(above) African Americans could now go to school in the South. This photograph shows a science class at Tuskegee Institute in Alabama. (below) After the Civil War, African American men voted for the first time.

African Americans were poor. Few had money to buy land. Many of them went to work for other people. Many African Americans rented land from farmers. They were called **sharecroppers** because they paid their rent with a share of their crops. They often had to borrow cash to buy things they needed.

Although Reconstruction was a difficult time, some good things did happen for African Americans. They were allowed to go to school. They were able to start their own businesses. New laws allowed African American men to vote. Some were elected to state governments and even to Congress.

In 1877, Congress took the Army out of the South. This was the official end of Reconstruction. But bad feelings from the war remained. Some white Southerners formed secret groups like the Ku Klux Klan. They used violence to keep African Americans from voting and from having equal rights.

Slavery was over. But it would take about 100 years before African Americans would begin to be treated as the equals of other Americans.

 **How do you think African Americans felt about Reconstruction?**

After the Civil War, freed slaves still had many problems. Most Southerners did not want to treat people who had been their slaves as equals. Most African Americans had never gone to school. They did not know how to read or write. Almost all former slaves were poor. They did not have jobs.

In 1865, the United States Congress decided that African Americans in the South needed help. So Congress stepped in and set up the Freedmen's Bureau. This government agency gave food, clothing, and fuel to poor people. It helped former slaves find jobs. It helped them understand written agreements about jobs. The Freedmen's Bureau set up hospitals and law courts.

The Freedmen's Bureau also built more than 4,300 schools and hired teachers to educate the freed slaves. It went on protecting the rights of African Americans until 1872.

**Why do you think education was so important for the freed slaves?**

_____

Both children and adults went to this Southern free school.

**Complete each sentence. Circle the letter in front of the correct answer.**

1. In a civil war
   a. people from the same country fight one another.
   b. people from the East fight people from the West.
   c. soldiers set up blockades.
   d. African Americans fight for the North.

2. The 11 Southern states that formed their own nation were called
   a. the Southern States of America.
   b. the Union.
   c. the Confederate States of America.
   d. the United Southern States.

3. The early battles of the Civil War were won by the South because
   a. it had more soldiers.
   b. its factories produced more guns.
   c. it blockaded Northern ports.
   d. it had better generals.

4. The Emancipation Proclamation
   a. freed the slaves in the South.
   b. was an important award.
   c. was an early battle of the Civil War.
   d. created free schools for slaves.

5. One result of the Civil War was that
   a. Lincoln became President.
   b. 11 Southern states left the Union.
   c. there were more plantations in the South.
   d. slavery was ended in the United States.

6. The years between 1865 and 1877 were called
   a. the Battle of Gettysburg.
   b. Reconstruction.
   c. the Civil War.
   d. the Lincoln Years.

**THINKING AND WRITING** Why do you think that many Southerners did not want to give equal rights to African Americans after the Civil War?

_____

_____

_____

_____

_____

_____

# Reading a Double Bar Graph

You have learned that at the time of the Civil War, the North had more miles of railroad track than the South. The double bar graph below compares the North and the South at the beginning of the Civil War.

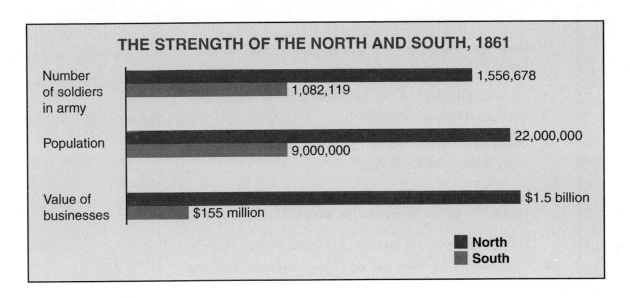

**THE STRENGTH OF THE NORTH AND SOUTH, 1861**

Number of soldiers in army — North: 1,556,678 — South: 1,082,119

Population — North: 22,000,000 — South: 9,000,000

Value of businesses — North: $1.5 billion — South: $155 million

■ North
■ South

1. Which side had the largest population?

   _____

2. Which side had businesses that were more valuable?

   _____

3. How many more soldiers were in the Union (North) Army than the Confederate (South) Army?

   _____

4. Which side do you think was stronger at the beginning of the Civil War? Use the information from the bar graphs to explain your answer.

   _____

   _____

   _____

Now it's time to finish your unit project. Think about what you learned about inventions of the 1800s. Talk with your team about answers to questions like these.

- **How was the cotton gin a helpful invention for the South? How did it work?**

- **How might events have been different if the cotton gin had not been invented?**

- **What new factory machines made goods that were used during the Civil War?**

- **How did the other inventions you learned about make life better or worse for people?**

Decide how you want to show the results of your project. Choose one of these ways or use one of your own ideas.

➤ Make diagrams of the cotton gin showing how it works. Make diagrams of several other inventions you learned about. Use your diagrams to make a bulletin board display. Add captions that explain how the inventions changed life for Americans.

➤ Describe the cotton gin and the other inventions as if you were selling them in a TV commercial—in the 1800s. Explain how they work. Tell your audience how they will change their lives. Make a product brochure to hand out to your "customers." If possible, videotape your commercials.

# UNIT 5

# The Nation Grows

In this unit you will read about a time when the United States grew. Immigrants came to the United States, hoping for a better life. They brought with them many different beliefs and customs. Farming and ranching became big businesses. The United States won a war and gained new lands.

But American Indians were forced to leave their lands. Laws were needed to protect the rights of children, workers, and the poor. In Europe, a war began.

Unit 5 will help you find answers to questions like these about our nation.

- How did Jane Addams help the poor?

- What happened to the American Indians?

- Who were the Rough Riders?

## UNIT PROJECT

Start a team project. Find out more about how the United States improved and grew stronger, during the late 1800s and early 1900s. Choose events that you think show this progress. Arrange them into a Time Line of Progress, 1860–1918.

# Industry and Immigrants, 1870–1910

In this chapter, you'll read about two important parts of the American story—industry and immigrants. It was a time of new inventions. It was also a time of many changes in how people lived.

 **Choose one invention shown on this page and tell how it made life easier or better.**

_____

_____

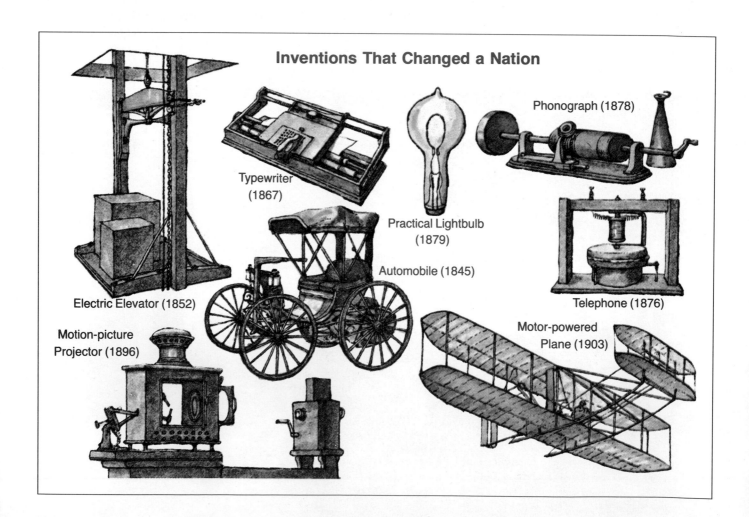

**Inventions That Changed a Nation**

Typewriter (1867)

Phonograph (1878)

Practical Lightbulb (1879)

Automobile (1845)

Telephone (1876)

Electric Elevator (1852)

Motion-picture Projector (1896)

Motor-powered Plane (1903)

## Steel and "Black Glue"

Do you know what buildings, automobiles, bridges, and bicycles all have in common? They are made partly of steel. One important new invention was a cheaper way to make steel. Before the Civil War, iron was used for many things. Steel is made from iron with other metals added. But steel is stronger and lasts longer than iron.

Many new inventions used steel. Tall buildings many stories high, called skyscrapers, were made of steel. The automobile had a steel frame. Barbed wire made of steel was used to fence cattle ranches. Steel also became the new material for older inventions. Bridges were made of iron and steel instead of wood. These bridges could carry trains across wide rivers like the Mississippi and the Ohio.

New uses for steel brought many new uses for oil. At first, people didn't think oil was good for much. People digging wells for water sometimes found oil instead. They called it "black glue." Soon people discovered that oil could be used to make other goods—like gasoline and kerosene. Before electricity, kerosene was used to light lamps. Oil also heated new city skyscrapers. It ran big machines in factories. It ran trains. People now called oil "black gold."

**Gasoline was needed for one important new invention. What was it?**

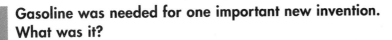

The inventions meant new factories. People moved to cities to work in the factories. Cities kept growing. Some cities became known for special products. Glass was made in Corning, New York. Cereal came from Battle Creek, Michigan.

In the 1800s, oil was pumped out of oil fields in Pennsylvania, Kentucky, Ohio, Illinois, and Indiana. Later, oil also flowed from Texas, California, and Oklahoma.

Steel was strong enough to support large railroad bridges.

Ships sailed from Europe crowded with immigrants.

## A Nation of Immigrants

Factories helped cities grow. So did the arrival of **immigrants.** An immigrant is a person who leaves one country to live in another country. Immigrants came from countries in Europe such as Italy, Greece, Poland, Ireland, Sweden, and Russia. They came from China in Asia. They came from countries to the south like Mexico. Most immigrants sailed across oceans on crowded ships.

 **Which immigrant groups used ships to travel to the United States? Which groups probably did not?**

Some immigrants came only to work and save money. They planned to return to their homelands. Others said good-bye to their homelands for good.

Why did these immigrants decide to leave their homelands? They left because they were poor and hungry. They left to get away from cruel and unfair laws. They left to start a new life.

To the immigrants, America was a land of hope. There was the promise of a better life. There were jobs. There was plenty of cheap land. There was freedom of religion.

**Look at the graph below. A line graph like this shows how something changes over time. This one shows the number of immigrants who came to this country between 1820 and 1929. Between what years did the largest number of immigrants come? How many came during those years?**

These immigrants work in a shop under very difficult conditions.

## A New Life

Immigrants arrived feeling very hopeful. But life in the new land wasn't easy. There were strange sights and sounds. People had to learn new skills to get jobs. Some farmers, for example, had to learn to work in factories. Sometimes teachers went to work in stores.

Many immigrants did not know English. That made many simple things difficult. It was hard for people who did not understand the language to buy food at a store, find the way to an office, or learn things at school.

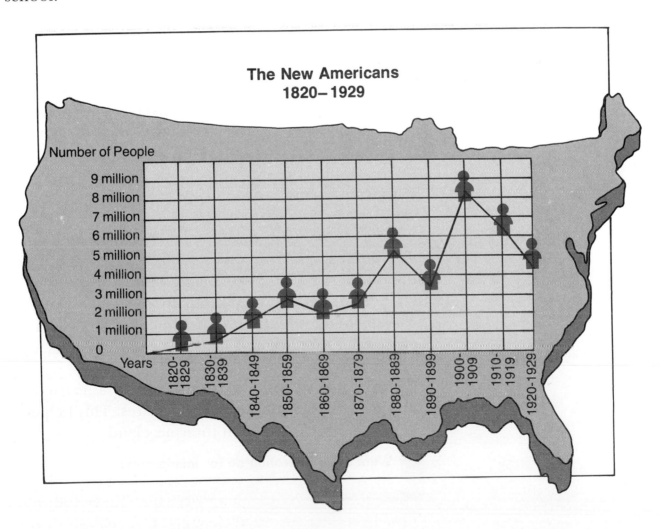

**The New Americans**
**1820–1929**

127

This picture of a New York City tenement was taken in 1910.

Some Americans who were born in the United States were not friendly to immigrants. These Americans were afraid immigrants would take their jobs. They thought immigrants would have a hard time living in a free land and following its laws.

## A Hard Life

Worst of all, immigrants often lived in the poorest part of a city. They lived in buildings called **tenements.** Tenements were put up quickly and cheaply. They were dark and had narrow hallways. They had bad lighting and caught fire easily. Whole families often lived crowded into one small room.

But the immigrants worked hard and were able to take on the ways of their new country. They were eager for education for themselves and their children. They felt education would help them do well in the United States. Schools were places where immigrants could learn about America and share their own cultures with others.

As they learned new ways, most immigrants tried to keep parts of their old lives and cultures. This helped them feel more at home in their new land.

**What could education do for immigrants?**

128

Groups of immigrants from the same country often settled in the same neighborhoods. In their homes and neighborhoods, they spoke their own languages and ate their own food. They followed their own religions and celebrated their holidays. The combination of cultures that immigrants brought with them has made the United States a very special nation.

**What did immigrants do to keep their cultures?**

_____

Immigrants from one country often formed groups to help new arrivals find work and places to live. Some immigrants opened shops to sell goods other immigrants needed, like clothing and food. Others opened restaurants and barbershops. People sold many things on the street. That way, they didn't need to rent a shop. All they needed was a pushcart.

As cities grew, so did the problems. Tenements and factories were built side by side. People had to live with noise, dirt, smoke, and bad air. There was nowhere safe to put garbage and other waste. Sometimes it was dumped into the same water people drank. This made people sick.

This street in New York City is full of activity. The street is crowded with people and pushcarts.

There weren't enough open places in the poor parts of the city. As you can see in the picture below, children often had to play in alleys.

## Work

Many children did not get a chance to play at all. They had to work long hours in factories. Sometimes they made only 25 cents a day. In 1906, two million children worked in factories. They had little or no time for play or school.

The factories were often terrible places to work. People worked from 12 to 14 hours a day, six days a week. Factories were dangerous and unhealthy. They were crowded, dark, and noisy. Accidents were common. Factories often caught fire.

**What was life like for factory workers?**

## Labor Unions Are Formed

Many workers wanted better pay and shorter hours. They wanted to work in a safe place.

Workers got together and formed **labor unions.** Labor unions are groups of workers who join together to protect their jobs and to improve working conditions. Factory owners were against unions. They believed workers had no right to ask for things like better pay.

(below, left) A child takes a bath in a tenement apartment. (below, right) These children are playing stickball, a kind of baseball.

Unions made the factory owners listen to the demands of workers. Unions did this by **striking,** or refusing to work, until changes were made. Unions were strong because all their members acted together. If one worker refused to work, a factory owner would just fire the worker. If a whole factory full of workers stopped working, it meant a loss of money and time for the owner. This threat might make the owner listen.

**Why were unions able to make factory owners listen to the demands of workers?**

(above) Factory work was hard and dangerous. (below) This child worked long hours in a factory.

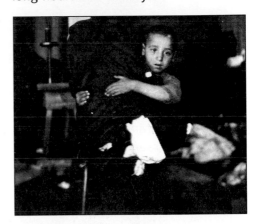

Sometimes factory owners tried to keep workers from joining unions or hired new workers during a strike. Both owners and unions even used violence to get their own way.

One of the most important unions was the American Federation of Labor (AFL). It was started by Samuel Gompers in 1886. By 1914 it had more than two million members.

But unions did help workers. They forced factory owners to stop hiring children. Because of unions, safety laws were passed. In some states, workers who were hurt on the job could get help.

UNIT PROJECT Tip

Work with your team to find out about some events in the history of labor unions. You may want to use them in your Time Line of Progress.

# Settlement Houses

City life was hard for poor immigrants. To help, some people opened **settlement houses** in poor parts of town. Settlement houses were neighborhood centers where people could go for help.

 **Why were settlement houses usually in poorer parts of town?**

---

(above) Jane Addams started Hull House. (below) Many children used the playground at Henry Street Settlement House.

Settlement houses had schools for young children. They had libraries and playgrounds. Doctors and nurses there helped the sick. People could learn new skills there. They could learn to read or to play an instrument.

In 1889, Jane Addams started the Hull House settlement in Chicago, Illinois. She helped many immigrants learn English. A few years later, Lillian Wald opened the Henry Street Settlement House in New York City. She showed parents how to keep their children healthy.

# CHAPTER ✔ CHECKUP

**Complete each sentence. Circle the letter in front of the correct answer.**

1. Skyscrapers could be built because of the invention of
   a. steel.
   b. gasoline.
   c. iron.
   d. railroads.

2. Oil
   a. is made with iron and other metals.
   b. was called "black water."
   c. was sold from a pushcart.
   d. ran big factory machines.

3. Most immigrants to the United States
   a. came here by train.
   b. did not understand English.
   c. wanted to forget their old culture.
   d. were very lazy.

4. Cities grew because
   a. land was cheap.
   b. tenements were very crowded.
   c. more people came to work in the factories.
   d. people sold goods from pushcarts.

5. Tenements were
   a. small schools.
   b. places to buy food.
   c. crowded apartment buildings that were dark and caught fire easily.
   d. built by the people who lived there.

6. Labor unions
   a. had dangerous machines.
   b. helped protect the workers.
   c. were safe factories.
   d. hired children to work in factories.

**THINKING AND WRITING**

Why did immigrants come to the United States?

_____

_____

_____

_____

_____

_____

_____

_____

# CHAPTER 13

# The Closing of the Frontier, 1860–1890

In the last chapter, you read about the growth of our nation's cities after the Civil War. In this chapter, you will learn what happened outside the cities during that time.

You will read about the frontier—the large, open spaces of our country. You will find out about the American Indian people who had lived there for hundreds of years. And you will learn about the settlers who moved to the frontier.

## Railroads Change the Frontier

The most important change on the frontier was the building of railroads. Railroads made it possible for more people to reach the frontier. Railroads made it possible for crops to be sent back to the East and for tools to be sent to the West. Railroads made it possible for cities and industry to develop where none had been before.

 **How do people travel great distances today?**

_____

Trains made travel by covered wagon a thing of the past.

134

# A Transcontinental Railroad Is Built

For a long time, people wanted a transcontinental railroad—one that would join the eastern and western parts of the North American continent. In 1862, Congress gave two companies money and land to build a railroad. A railroad already ran from the East Coast to Omaha, Nebraska. So the Union Pacific Railroad would build west from Omaha. The Central Pacific Railroad Company would build east from Sacramento, California.

The two railroad lines met in May 1869, after several years of hard work. The people who had worked to build the railroad held a celebration. They joined the eastern and western lines of track with a golden spike. Now it would only take about a week to carry raw materials and products across the continent. Now travelers could leave one coast on a Monday and see the other coast seven days later.

**On the map below, purple lines show other railroads in the United States. Trace the routes of the Central Pacific and the Union Pacific railroads from Sacramento to Omaha. Circle Promontory, the city in Utah, where the two new railroads met.**

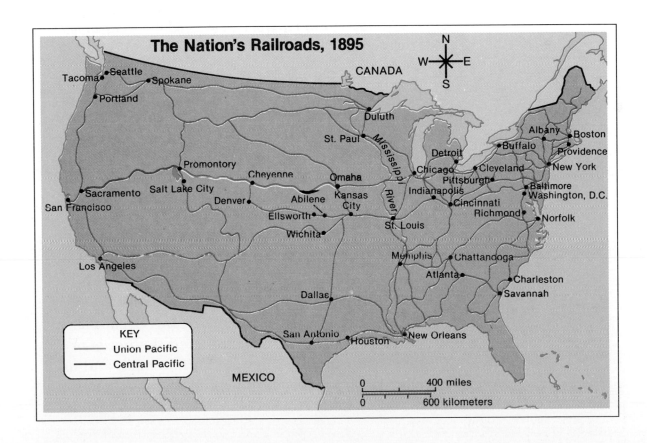

## The Nation's Railroads, 1895

Seattle, Tacoma, Spokane, Portland, CANADA, Duluth, St. Paul, Albany, Boston, Buffalo, Providence, Detroit, Cleveland, New York, Promontory, Cheyenne, Omaha, Chicago, Pittsburgh, Salt Lake City, Indianapolis, Baltimore, Sacramento, Denver, Abilene, Kansas City, Cincinnati, Washington, D.C., San Francisco, Ellsworth, St. Louis, Richmond, Norfolk, Wichita, Memphis, Chattanooga, Los Angeles, Atlanta, Charleston, Dallas, Savannah, San Antonio, New Orleans, Houston, MEXICO, Mississippi River

KEY
— Union Pacific
— Central Pacific

0 — 400 miles
0 — 600 kilometers

The American Indians of the Great Plains depended on buffalo for food, clothing, and other needs.

Most of the workers for the Union Pacific were Irish immigrants or African Americans. Many of the workers for the Central Pacific were Chinese immigrants.

It was not easy building a transcontinental railroad. The Chinese immigrants had to dig tunnels through the mountains known as the Sierra Nevadas in California. At this time, there were no power shovels. Workers had no dynamite to blast away the rock. The workers dug the tunnels with hand tools—shovels and picks. One tunnel was only a quarter of a mile long. But it took a full year to dig.

 **Why was it hard for workers to build the transcontinental railroad?**

Scouts were posted to protect the workers from American Indians. The American Indians were angry about the railroad crossing their lands.

## Lives of the American Indians

American Indians lived on the land between the Mississippi River and the Rocky Mountains long before railroads and settlers from the United States went there. This region is called the Great Plains.

Most of the American Indians of the Great Plains did not farm or ranch. They followed the herds of buffalo each summer. They ate buffalo meat and used buffalo skins to make clothing and blankets. They used buffalo bones for tools.

(above, left) This Navajo woman named Juanita went to Washington, D.C., with other American Indians in 1874. They tried to make peace between their people and the United States government. (above, right) Chief Joseph was a famous American Indian leader.

The American Indians' way of life was changed after the railroads arrived. American Indians killed only as many buffalo as they could use for food and other things. But hunters from the eastern United States came to kill as many buffalo as they could. They sent the skins back to the East on the railroads. They made money by selling the skins.

In a few years, millions of buffalo were killed. By 1889, only about 1,000 were left. That meant the American Indians who lived on the plains had no steady supply of food.

The American Indians also lost the land they lived on. As settlers moved west, the government of the United States made the American Indians move away. But the American Indians did not give up their lands easily. They fought the settlers and the soldiers. In the end, however, the American Indians had to give up or keep getting defeated by soldiers.

**What happened to the American Indians of the Great Plains when the buffalo were killed by hunters from the East?**

The American Indians were forced to move to reservations. Only American Indians lived there. The lands were in places that settlers did not want to have.

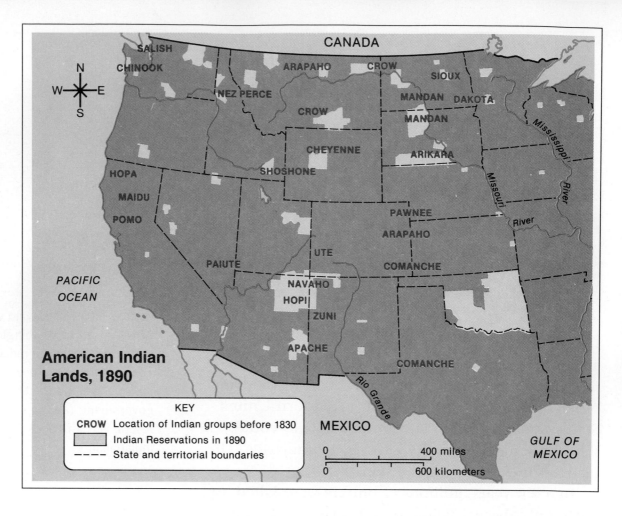

American Indian Lands, 1890

KEY
CROW Location of Indian groups before 1830
Indian Reservations in 1890
- - - - State and territorial boundaries

0      400 miles
0   600 kilometers

Life on the reservations could be very hard. Sometimes American Indian groups were forced to live on reservations far from the land where they once had lived. People who had spent their lives following the buffalo across the plains now had to live in one place. Hunters had to learn to farm in order to get food. And the soil was usually not good for farming. For the people on the reservations, life meant poverty and sickness. At the time when Columbus visited America, there may have been one million American Indians. By 1900, there were only 237,000.

Today, the number of American Indians has grown. Many live outside the reservations. But many continue to live on reservations. There they keep their old ways of life and cultures alive.

 Look at the map of American Indian Lands in 1890. Find the largest reservation on the map and circle it. In what state is it located?

These settlers had been slaves before the Civil War. Now they were homesteaders.

## Homesteaders Settle on the Great Plains

One of the last frontiers in the United States was the Great Plains. Now that railroads were there, people were able to settle there and start farms.

Life on the plains was very hard. The weather is very cold in the winter and very hot in the summer. The land is covered by tough grass, and there are almost no trees.

Why did people move to the Great Plains? Most of them wanted to have farms of their own. The railroad companies wanted more business, so they tried to get people to settle there.

The government also wanted people to go to the Great Plains. In 1862, Congress passed the Homestead Act. This law gave land on the Great Plains to anyone who was willing to live and farm on it for five years. The people who did this were called **homesteaders.** Many people went to the frontier because they did not have enough money to buy land in the East.

 **What might you have taken with you if you had been a homesteader?**

 The Homestead Act is important for your Time Line of Progress. Remember that some progress took place over periods of time without exact dates. Figure out a way to show these changes on your time line.

Because there were no trees for lumber, the early settlers had to build their homes from **sod.** Sod is hard soil held together by grass. The settlers cut sod into large blocks.

There are very few rivers on the Great Plains. Farmers had to dig deep wells to reach water. Sometimes they had to go down as far as 300 feet.

## Farming Becomes Big Business

New machines were needed to farm on the Great Plains. The thick sod was too tough and sticky for ordinary plows. A man named John Deere made a new kind of plow with a very sharp steel blade. He also made a plow that farmers could ride on. Other new machines made it easier to harvest the crops.

These machines made it possible for one person to do much more work than before. The farms of the Great Plains grew bigger and bigger. The first farmers had raised only enough food for their own families. But by the early 1900s, farming had become a big business. Many farmers raised only one crop—usually wheat—and sold it to food companies. Wheat farmers depended on the railroads to ship their wheat to buyers.

(above) The grass on the roof of this sod house is still growing. (below) Machines like this helped farmers grow more wheat on the Great Plains.

 **How did machines help farmers on the Great Plains?**

_____

**140**

## The Cowboys

By the early 1800s, settlers from the United States had started living on the Texas plains. They started ranches with wild cattle they found on the plains. The people who worked on the ranches were called **cowboys.**

Many of the cowboys were Mexicans. They stayed in Texas after Texas became independent from Mexico. About a quarter of the cowboys were African Americans. Some had come to the West after the Civil War. Others had been slaves on Texas ranches.

One of the cowboys' jobs was to keep the cattle from leaving the ranches. There were no fences to keep the cattle there. In the summer, the cowboys would round up the cattle and move them to a railroad town. From there, the cattle were sent to cities in the East.

There were no railroads in Texas, so the cattle had to be moved all the way to Kansas. The **trail drive,** or trip to the railroad, usually took about two or three months. Along the way, the cattle grazed freely on the open plains. By the end of the drive, the fattened cattle were ready for market.

By 1890 the railroads had reached Texas. Trail drives were no longer needed. At the same time, rich ranchers were buying up huge amounts of land. They built fences of barbed wire around their land. The plains were no longer open.

**Why do you think ranchers built barbed wire fences?**

_____

(above) An African American cowboy in the 1800s.

(below) Cowboys wore seatless trousers called chaps over their regular trousers. Chaps helped protect their legs from thorny brush and from rubbing during long hours in the saddle.

141

Chief Sitting Bull

Sitting Bull, or Tatanka Yotanka, was a leader of the American Indian group called the Sioux. He was upset about the number of settlers coming to live on the Great Plains. Sitting Bull and some other American Indian leaders decided to fight for their land. They attacked wagon trains and fought the United States Army for many years.

Then, in 1868, the United States made peace with the Sioux. The U.S. government agreed that the Sioux owned the land called the Black Hills in the state of South Dakota. But, in 1874, General George Custer ignored the treaty and led government troops into the Black Hills. Custer led a team studying minerals in the area. Gold was later discovered there. Soon other people came to dig for gold.

The government wanted the valuable land. But the Sioux refused to let the United States buy the land. Once again the Sioux were forced off their land.

Sitting Bull and other American Indian leaders decided to fight for their land. One of the last battles took place in 1876. General Custer and all his men were killed. This battle has become known as "Custer's Last Stand."

This was a great victory for the Sioux. But it was also their last. A very large army was sent to fight the Sioux. Many of the American Indian leaders decided not to fight.

Sitting Bull escaped to Canada. He stayed there for several years. In 1881 he returned to the United States. Sitting Bull spent most of the rest of his life on a reservation in South Dakota. The government feared that Sitting Bull would start an uprising among the Sioux. In 1890, American Indian police officers were sent to arrest Sitting Bull. In the process, he was killed.

**Why did Sitting Bull tell his people to fight?**

# CHAPTER ✓ CHECKUP

**Complete each sentence. Circle the letter in front of the correct answer.**

1.  The transcontinental railroad joined
    **a.** the North and the South.
    **b.** the mountains and the Pacific Ocean.
    **c.** the East and the West.
    **d.** the forests and the Great Plains.

2.  The buffalo were important to the
    **a.** settlers.
    **b.** railroad builders.
    **c.** American Indians.
    **d.** United States Army.

3.  On reservations, American Indians
    **a.** lived the way they always had.
    **b.** had good soil for farming.
    **c.** made lots of money.
    **d.** often had to learn how to farm.

4.  The Homestead Act gave
    **a.** land to settlers.
    **b.** land to American Indians.
    **c.** Sitting Bull a place to live.
    **d.** farming equipment to settlers.

5.  New farm machines made it possible
    **a.** for railroads to cross the Great Plains.
    **b.** for one person to do a lot more work.
    **c.** for hunters to kill buffalo.
    **d.** for cowboys to work on ranches.

6.  The trail drive was how
    **a.** cowboys got cattle to the railroads.
    **b.** the Army moved American Indians to reservations.
    **c.** the settlers got to the Great Plains.
    **d.** farmers took grain to market.

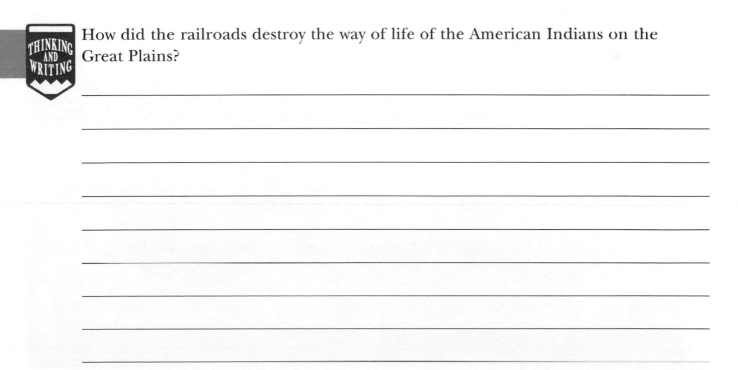

THINKING AND WRITING    How did the railroads destroy the way of life of the American Indians on the Great Plains?

_____

_____

_____

_____

_____

_____

_____

# CHAPTER 14

# A New America, 1898–1918

The United States was born in 1776 and "grew up" in the 1800s. By the end of the 1800s, the country had grown from 13 states to 45. It was strong and rich.

Between 1898 and 1918, Americans began working to make life better for poor people, children, and workers.

During these years, the United States fought two wars. These were the first wars the United States had fought outside its own borders.

 **How many more states do we have now than at the end of the 1800s?**

Armies still used horses in 1898.

## War with Spain

Earlier, the United States did not have much to do with the problems or wars of other countries. All that changed in 1898 when the United States went to war with Spain.

Cuba is an island near Florida. Columbus had claimed it for Spain in 1492. It was still a Spanish colony 400 years later. But some of the people of Cuba were fighting for independence from Spain.

United States President William McKinley did not want the country to fight in Cuba. But some American newspapers printed stories about how badly Spain treated its colonists. Many people felt we should help Cuba become free.

In 1898, the President sent the battleship *Maine* to protect Americans who lived in Cuba. One night the *Maine* blew up in a terrible explosion. More than 250 American sailors were killed. The United States blamed Spain for the explosion, and a war with Spain began. It was called the Spanish-American War.

 **Find Cuba on the map. Why do you think the United States might worry about a war in Cuba?**

_____

_____

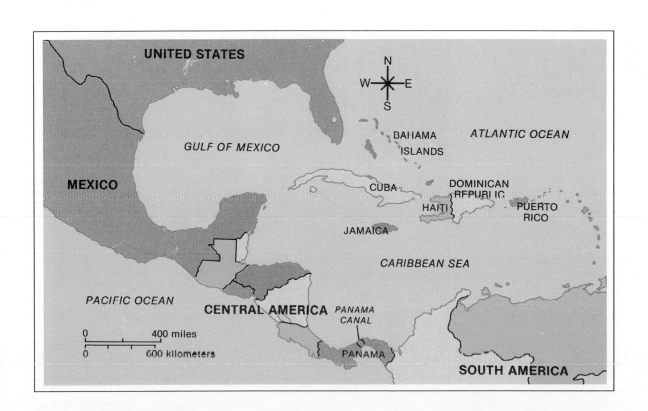

The United States won the Spanish-American War quickly. As a result of the war, Spain had to give some islands that it ruled to the United States. These included the Philippine Islands and Guam, in the Pacific Ocean, and Puerto Rico in the Atlantic.

One of the men who fought in Cuba was Theodore (Teddy) Roosevelt. He was the leader of a group of **cavalry,** soldiers who rode horses. His group, the Rough Riders, became famous during the Spanish-American War. In 1901, when President McKinley was killed, Vice President Teddy Roosevelt became President of the United States.

 **Why do you think the American soldiers in Cuba rode horses?**

## The Progressive Era

Although America was a rich country, most of its citizens were not rich. People who worked on farms and in factories made very little money. Some of the machines they used were dangerous. Workers could be badly hurt. And many of the workers were children.

These children worked many hours in a mine six days a week. They saw daylight only on Sundays.

Unions were formed to solve these problems, but they were only able to make some things better. Unions could only help their members. And many people worked in places that had no unions.

How was it possible that ten-year-old children were made to work in mines and factories? Why did workers have to use machines that might kill them? Why weren't there any laws to protect these people?

There were many reasons why people were not protected at work. One reason was that Americans still liked to think of themselves as pioneers. They believed that people should take care of themselves. They thought that if someone did not like a job, that person should find another job. A person who was sick or poor should ask family or friends for help.

But things were not that simple anymore. Most people could not get in a covered wagon and find a better place to live. By 1900, most Americans lived in cities. There weren't enough jobs, so people took what they could get. And poor families had to send their children to work.

**Why did people work at unsafe and low-paying jobs?**

This young girl worked in a cotton factory.

The **Progressives** were a group of Americans who believed there should be laws to protect people. The Progressives came from many political groups. It wasn't just children and the poor that they were trying to protect. They believed life could be improved for all Americans. They wanted all people—not just the rich and powerful—to take part in running the government. During these years women began to gain more political power. Many states in the West and Midwest gave women the right to vote.

UNIT
**PROJECT**
Tip

Find out more about some of the important laws Congress passed during the Progressive Era to make life better for all Americans.

Progressives also wanted to protect the health of Americans. In 1906, Progressive writer Upton Sinclair wrote a book called *The Jungle*. The story was about unhealthful conditions in the meat-packing business. Meat was not being prepared in a healthful way.

After President Roosevelt read *The Jungle,* he urged Congress to pass laws about how meat and other foods should be prepared. Today, the government checks to make sure food companies prepare foods the right way.

The Progressives got the government to change many other laws. Factories became safer. Children received better protection. So many laws were passed at that time that the years from 1898 to 1918 are now known as the Progressive Era.

**What was the book *The Jungle* about?**

_____

_____

Upton Sinclair (above) wrote about unhealthful conditions in meat-packing businesses like this sausage factory (right).

## A World War

In the early 1900s, Europe was made up of nations that were jealous and afraid of each other. Groups of nations had agreed to help if any one of them was attacked. For this reason, in the summer of 1914, a war between two countries spread to most of the nations of Europe. On one side were the **Allies.** The most important Allies were Great Britain, France, and Russia. On the other side were the **Central Powers.** These included Austria-Hungary and Germany. The nations that did not enter the war were called **neutral.**

 **Look at the map below. On which side were most of the nations of Europe?**

_____

In the summer of 1914, most Americans were not interested in the war. Europe was far away. It took six days to get there by ship, and not many people could afford to go.

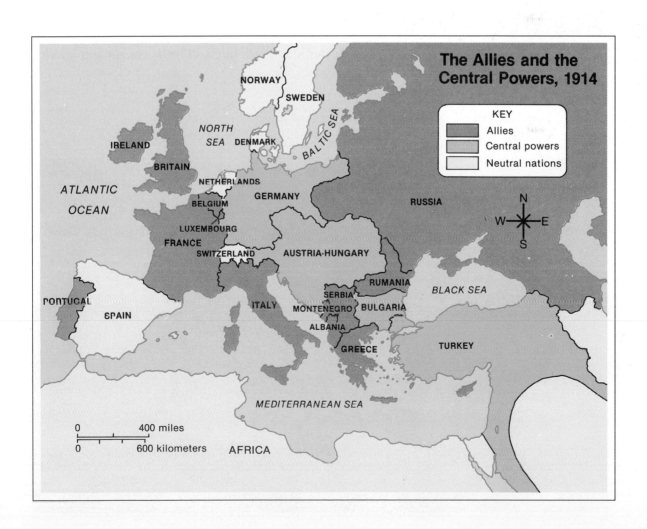

The Allies and the Central Powers, 1914

KEY
Allies
Central powers
Neutral nations

## The United States and World War I

The United States was neutral for the first three years of the war. During that time, German submarines were sinking British ships that were not part of the war. In 1915, the Germans sank the ocean liner *Lusitania.* Most of the people on board died. More than one hundred of them were Americans.

In 1917, the Germans said they would sink any American ship going to Great Britain. President Woodrow Wilson asked Congress to declare war against the Central Powers.

American soldiers reached Europe in June 1917. The Allies were very glad to see the Yanks, as the Americans were called. The Allies needed help from the Yanks and more soldiers to fight.

Both sides in the war had dug long trenches in the battlefields. The soldiers lived and fought in the trenches. Many men were killed each time one side tried to attack the other side. On one day, 60,000 British soldiers died.

In November 1918, World War I was over. The Allies won.

 **Why do you think soldiers lived in trenches during World War I?**

(above) Posters like this one reminded Americans that everyone had to help win the war. (below) During the war, soldiers lived in muddy trenches like this one for several weeks at a time.

150

(above) These soldiers are waving good-bye to France as they sail home after World War I. (below) During the war, women did jobs that men used to do.

## After the War

War can change countries in many ways. Many homes were destroyed during the fighting in France and Germany. The United States changed, too, but in different ways. During World War I, Americans had learned about new ways to live.

Before the war, many women worked at home. But there were many new jobs during the war, and not enough men to do them. Women went to work in factories making things the soldiers needed.

**What kinds of goods would the Army and Navy need?**

_____

_____

Women proved that they could do the same jobs as men. They wanted the same rights, too. In many states, they did not have the right to vote. Women worked hard to change this. In 1920, the 19th Amendment gave women the right to vote.

Some African Americans fought in the war. Many others moved to the northeast to work in factories there. Life there was a little better for the African Americans, but they still did not have equal rights.

**151**

# The Panama Canal

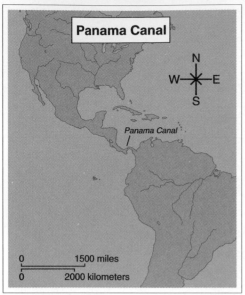

**Panama Canal**

N
W—E
S

Panama Canal

| | |
|---|---|
| 0 | 1500 miles |
| 0 | 2000 kilometers |

During the war with Spain, the United States sent a battleship from California to Cuba. The ship sailed all the way around South America. This trip was 13,000 miles. After the war, Congress decided to build a canal so battleships could get from the Pacific Ocean to the Atlantic Ocean quickly.

The United States built the canal in the country of Panama in Central America. It was a difficult job. The weather was always hot and damp. Workers died from diseases carried by mosquitoes.

Miles of canal had to be dug through thick jungle. Landslides often filled the holes that workers dug. Huge amounts of earth had to be carried away— enough to fill a train of railroad cars that could wrap around the world four times! No wonder people thought the canal an example of great engineering.

More than 43,000 people worked on the Panama Canal. It was almost 51 miles long. It was finished in 1914. It had taken ten years to build.

This picture was taken while workers were still digging the Panama Canal. The canal had to be very wide and very deep so that large ships could sail through it. The Panama Canal shortened sea travel between the Atlantic and Pacific oceans.

**About 37 ships go through the Panama Canal every day. How many ships go through the canal in one year?**

# CHAPTER ✓ CHECKUP

**Complete each sentence. Circle the letter in front of the correct answer.**

1. The battleship *Maine* was sent to Cuba by President McKinley to
   a. fight the Spanish.
   b. protect Americans in Cuba.
   c. deliver supplies to the Cubans.
   d. explode in the harbor.

2. The Progressives wanted laws to
   a. make children work in mines.
   b. become President.
   c. have people live in cities.
   d. protect everyone.

3. Nations that do not enter or take sides in a war are called
   a. Progressives.
   b. neutral.
   c. Allies.
   d. brave.

4. The United States entered World War I because
   a. the Germans said they would sink American ships.
   b. the British were losing the war.
   c. Austria-Hungary tried to become neutral.
   d. the President tried to change the laws.

5. America entered World War I in
   a. 1898.
   b. 1914.
   c. 1917.
   d. 1920.

6. In World War I, the Americans fought against the
   a. Spanish.
   b. Cubans.
   c. Central Powers.
   d. Allies.

**THINKING AND WRITING**

How did World War I change the lives of women in the United States?

_____

_____

_____

_____

_____

_____

_____

# Reading a Line Graph

During the years between 1900 and 1920, labor union membership grew. Unions held many strikes to help workers gain more rights. Slowly, conditions in factories improved as workers fought together for better pay, a shorter workday, and a safer place to work.

1. About how many workers belonged to a labor union in 1900? Circle the correct answer.

   less than 1,000,000   exactly 1,000,000   more than 1,000,000

2. Did membership increase or decrease between 1900 and 1905?

   _____

3. During what years did membership stay about the same?

   _____

4. About how many people belonged to labor unions in 1920?

   _____

5. How does this line graph show that labor unions helped workers get things like better pay and a shorter workday?

   _____

   _____

Now it's time to finish your unit project. Think about progress made in the United States between 1860 and 1918. Talk with your team about answers to questions like these.

- **What were some important events that showed progress during this time?**

- **What was some important progress made by labor unions?**

- **What periods of time showed progress without exact dates?**

Decide how you want to make your Time Line of Progress. Choose one of these ideas or use one of your own ideas.

➤ Dramatize your time line. Have team members dress in costumes and act out each event you have chosen for the time line. Have them carry signs with dates and names of the events. One person can narrate the time line.

➤ Make a mural of your time line. Draw a line on a paper from a roll or several sheets joined together. Write the dates for the time line over the right place on the line. Write the events by the dates. Use colored markers and crayons to illustrate the time line.

# UNIT 6

# A World Power

After World War I the nations of Europe knew that the United States was now one of the most important countries of the world.

In the 1920s, the United States grew even stronger. Then, suddenly, everything changed. Factories closed. People lost their jobs and their homes. As the nation recovered, another world war began. But the United States kept on growing into an important world power.

In Unit 6 you will find answers to questions like these.

- What was the stock market crash?
- Who was Franklin Delano Roosevelt?
- How did African Americans win their civil rights?

## UNIT PROJECT

Start a team project. Find out about the different kinds of music that have been popular in the United States from the Jazz Age to the present. Listen to examples of the music. Learn about the people who made each kind of music popular.

# The Jazz Age and the Depression, 1920–1939

After World War I ended in 1918, the United States faced the future with hope. People were ready to enjoy peace and to make great changes in their lives. Young people especially wanted to be freer and have more fun. They dressed in new ways. They made dancing the "in" thing to do. A new kind of music called jazz filled the air.

Jazz was fast, loud, and different—just what young people loved. It mixed American tunes and African beats. African American musicians started playing jazz in New Orleans. During World War I, great musicians like Louis "Satchmo" Armstrong and Bessie Smith performed in jazz clubs. They made records. Soon people were listening to and dancing to jazz in all parts of the country.

**What was jazz like?**

(below, left) The 1920s were a time of change. Some women stopped wearing long dresses. (below, right) Bessie Smith was one of the great jazz and blues singers. Many fans of jazz and blues still listen to her records today.

In 1927, Charles Lindbergh was the first person to fly alone across the Atlantic Ocean. It took him over 33 hours.

## Life Gets Better

Some people listened to jazz on a new invention called the radio. By 1927, there were 700 radio stations with thousands of listeners. Stations hired bands to play music. They had comedy and mystery shows. Radio gave people the news almost as soon as it happened. They didn't have to wait for tomorrow's newspaper.

 **What do you think people did to hear music before radios and records?**

In the 1920s, Americans had more time to listen to the radio. Other new products were making their lives easier. Now they could buy electric refrigerators to keep foods fresh instead of using boxes with ice. There were machines to wash clothes. A few years before, shopping, cooking, cleaning, and washing had taken many hours every day. The new electric machines helped change this. Women who worked at home no longer had to work all day.

Women marched in parades to show they wanted to vote.

## Women and the Vote

In 1920, women won the right to vote. It was a right that they had tried to get for many years. In 1848, Elizabeth Cady Stanton became a leader in the movement for **suffrage.** Suffrage is the right to vote. For more than 70 years, women tried to get Congress to pass a law that would allow them to vote.

The western states were the first to give women suffrage. Women got the right to vote in Wyoming in 1869, even before it became a state. In fact, the government of Wyoming said it did not want to become a state if women were not allowed to vote.

When they won the vote, many women decided to turn away from old ways of doing things. They cut their hair and shortened their long skirts. They went dancing and listened to jazz. They decided to make more choices about how they would live their lives.

## America on Wheels

Henry Ford had a dream. He wanted to build a simple car that many people could afford. He called it the Model T. He built the first one in 1908. Because of Ford's dream, there were millions of cars on American roads by the 1920s.

Ford used an **assembly line** to make his cars. It was a moving belt that carried the cars past the workers. Each worker added a different part. A new car rolled off the Ford assembly line every ten seconds! A Model T cost less than $900. The assembly line speeded up production in factories. Soon other businesses made goods this way. The assembly line completely changed the way Americans made products.

Cars led to other businesses and new jobs. Roads had to be built. Tires and other auto parts were needed. Gasoline stations were needed. People could travel farther, so there were more restaurants, theaters, and hotels. People could drive to their jobs, so they did not have to live in cities.

**Name two ways in which the car changed life in the United States.**

_____

_____

(above) By the 1920s, there were already many cars in the United States. (below) Cars moved through the Ford factory on an assembly line. It took only two hours to put a car together.

# Farmers Have Problems

The United States grew quickly during the 1920s. Tractors and other machines made farming easier. Farmers planted larger crops. But soon the farmers found that they could not sell all their crops. There was so much food for sale that farmers had to lower the price of food. Many farmers had borrowed money to buy machines. Now they could not pay for them.

 **What did farmers have to do when there was too much food for sale?**

Farmers in the Great Plains had more problems. Cattle had eaten up all the grass in some places. This meant the wind could blow the bare soil away. The crops farmers planted in other places did not protect the soil from the wind. Little rain fell in the early 1930s, so crops did not grow. The soil began to dry up and blow away. Soon nothing was left but dust. Huge dust storms blew across the plains. Even the houses were filled with dust. The Great Plains was called by another name then—the Dust Bowl.

Many farmers gave up and moved away. They looked for jobs in the cities.

In Oklahoma the dry land turned to dust.

**UNIT PROJECT Tip**

With your team, learn about the music, such as the blues and some folk songs, that American people sang and listened to in hard times. Look for recordings by Woody Guthrie.

People had very little money during the Great Depression. Many people sold off whatever they could in order to buy food.

## The Great Depression

Like the farmers, factory owners of the 1920s also made more goods than people could buy. When the owners closed their factories, the workers lost their jobs. Because they had no money, the workers could not buy goods. That meant that more factories were closed and more workers lost their jobs.

In 1929, things got much worse. People all over the country had been buying small parts of businesses called **shares of stock.**

People buy and sell shares of stock to make money. They try to buy shares in a business at a low price. If the business does well, others will want to buy shares in it. Then the price of its shares will go higher. If the business does poorly, the price of its shares will fall. People try to sell shares for a higher price than they paid for them. If they do, they make money. Shares of stock are bought and sold in the **stock market.**

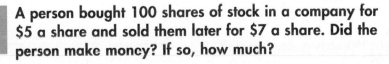

**A person bought 100 shares of stock in a company for $5 a share and sold them later for $7 a share. Did the person make money? If so, how much?**

In 1929, many people had bought shares of stock in many businesses. The prices of shares had soared. But when businesses made more goods than they could sell, they did badly or closed. Nobody wanted to buy shares of stock in them. So prices fell.

These families went to Washington, D.C., to ask the government to help them during the Great Depression.

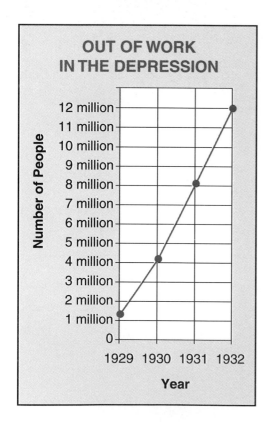

**OUT OF WORK IN THE DEPRESSION**

On October 29, 1929, a huge number of people decided to sell their shares before prices fell even lower. But no one was buying. On that day, prices of shares fell so low so fast that people said the stock market had crashed. Many people lost all their money.

People had borrowed money to buy shares. When the businesses closed, they could not pay back this money. Many banks had to close, too. People who had not borrowed money lost the money they had put in the banks.

All these events caused the period known as the Great **Depression.** A depression is a time when there is not enough money or work. People could not pay the money they owed on their homes. Thousands of people lost their homes. Many people had to eat at places called soup kitchens, where they lined up for free food.

**What is a depression?**

_____

_____

## Another Roosevelt Becomes President

The events of 1929 were only the beginning of America's problems. Over the next three years, thousands of banks and businesses closed. By 1932 one out of every four working adults did not have a job. Some men who had worked in offices had to sell apples or shine shoes on the street.

In the 1932 election, Americans voted for a new President. His name was Franklin Delano Roosevelt, but most people called him by his initials: FDR. He was a cousin of another President, Teddy Roosevelt.

As a young man, Roosevelt had studied law. Soon afterward he was chosen for a state government job in New York. Before he was 40 years old, he ran for Vice President of the United States. It was one of the few times he did not win.

Soon after this, something happened that changed Roosevelt's life. He got polio, a terrible sickness. He could no longer use his legs. But Roosevelt did not quit. He learned to walk with braces. And a few years later he was elected the governor of New York.

## A New Deal

When Franklin Roosevelt ran for President in 1932, he promised, "a new deal for the American people." This meant new laws and programs that would give people work. After Roosevelt was elected, more than four million people got jobs. They planted trees and built roads. They built dams that protected farms from floods. They worked for the government.

New laws were made. Some laws protected the money people put in banks. That way they would not lose it if the bank closed. People called these laws and programs the New Deal. The New Deal did not end the Great Depression, but it did help a lot of people who needed work.

Franklin D. Roosevelt talks to a voter.

**What was one way the New Deal helped people?**

163

# Life in the 1930s

The 1930s were hard times for most Americans. Things were getting better, but very slowly. Many Americans enjoyed listening to radio shows. Listening to the radio was a free way to have fun.

Movies were popular, too. The stories in the movies were more fun than real life was during the Depression. There was a new movie at every movie house twice every week. Before 1927, movies had no sound. But now there were "talkies," and some movies were even in color!

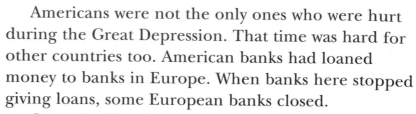

**Why did Americans love the movies?**

_____

_____

(above) The movie *The Wizard of Oz*, a popular musical fantasy, premiered August 18, 1939. (below) As part of the New Deal, people got jobs putting up schools and other buildings.

Americans were not the only ones who were hurt during the Great Depression. That time was hard for other countries too. American banks had loaned money to banks in Europe. When banks here stopped giving loans, some European banks closed.

Countries like Germany were very weak after World War I. These countries chose leaders who promised to make them strong again. Some leaders decided to do this by starting wars. If they won the wars, they could take the goods and resources of other countries.

After Franklin Delano Roosevelt was elected President in 1932, he made good use of the radio. He used it to explain the laws and programs of the New Deal. He called these radio talks "fireside chats." One young girl who listened to President Roosevelt's fireside chats lived in Hawaii. Her name was Patsy Takemoto. The President's talks made her want to help other people by working for the government.

In high school, Patsy won student elections. She stayed in Hawaii to go to college. Afterward she traveled to Chicago to study law. There she met and married John Mink. But her home in the beautiful islands of Hawaii called her back. For several years Patsy Takemoto Mink worked as a lawyer in Honolulu, Hawaii's capital.

Then she did what Franklin Roosevelt had done. She began to take part in the state government. Patsy won elections for several state government jobs. While she was a state senator, Hawaii became the fiftieth state.

Patsy Takemoto Mink

Patsy Takemoto Mink next turned her eye to the nation's government in Washington, D.C. Her husband and friends worked for nothing to help her get there. In 1964, she was elected to the United States Congress. In Congress she worked very hard to pass laws that would make life better for women, children, the poor, and the sick.

Although Patsy Takemoto Mink left Congress in 1977, she returned in 1992. She tried to protect the rights of all Americans, no matter what their race or culture. As a Hawaiian, she had learned to understand and value each culture. "What I bring to Congress," she said, "is a Hawaiian background of tolerance and equality." She died in 2002.

**What did Patsy Takemoto Mink think she could do if she worked for the government?**

# CHAPTER ✓ CHECKUP

**Complete each sentence. Circle the letter in front of the correct answer.**

1. Jazz music was
   a. invented by Bessie Smith.
   b. first played in Hawaii.
   c. not popular with young people.
   d. a mixture of African beats and American tunes.

2. In the 1920s, for the first time people got the news from
   a. radios.
   b. automobiles.
   c. airplanes.
   d. newspapers.

3. One of the first products to be made on an assembly line was the
   a. radio.
   b. car.
   c. highway.
   d. model airplane.

4. The Dust Bowl was
   a. a new kind of music played on the radio in the 1920s.
   b. the first radio station started in Pittsburgh.
   c. a name for the Great Plains in the 1930s when it did not rain.
   d. a yearly football game in Oklahoma.

5. A depression is a time when
   a. there is not enough money or work.
   b. a lot of dust appears.
   c. businesses make a lot of goods.
   d. the temperature rises.

6. Before Franklin Delano Roosevelt became President, he was
   a. the Vice President.
   b. a senator from Wyoming.
   c. a businessman.
   d. the governor of New York.

**THINKING AND WRITING**

What were some of the causes of the Great Depression?

_____

_____

_____

_____

_____

_____

_____

_____

# World War II, 1939–1945

In this chapter, you will read about the war that the United States fought with Germany, Japan, Italy, and other countries. World War II was a long war, and many people were killed.

## Before the War

By the 1930s, the Great Depression had hurt all the countries of Europe. At that time, Adolf Hitler became the leader of Germany. He was the leader of a group called the Nazis. After Germany lost World War I, it was poor and weak. Hitler promised to make Germany strong again.

**What did Hitler promise?**

_____

Hitler made many promises and got a lot of power. He used this power to become a **dictator.** A dictator is someone who has complete control of a country. No one is allowed to speak or act against a dictator.

The Germans got ready for another war. They began building many tanks like the ones shown here.

These concentration camp inmates were freed by the U.S. 7th Army in 1945. Unfortunately, most other prisoners of concentration camps were not so lucky.

Adolf Hitler became the dictator of Germany in the 1930s.

## The Holocaust

Adolf Hitler arrested many Jews. The Jews had done nothing wrong. They had a different religion than most Germans. Hitler blamed them for Germany's problems. He stirred up hatred against them.

The Jews and other people Hitler hated were put in prisons. These prisons were called **concentration camps.** Some Jews escaped Europe before they were put in the camps. But many could not escape. Six million Jews—men, women, and children—were murdered in the camps. Two out of every three Jews in Europe were killed. This terrible event is called the **Holocaust,** which means a total destruction.

**Why did Hitler arrest and kill Jews?**

_____

_____

## Getting Ready for War

To make Germany stronger, Hitler made the German army bigger. He had factories start making guns and other weapons.

Other countries had dictators, too. Benito Mussolini had become the dictator of Italy in the early 1920s. In Japan, army officers took over the government by the early 1940s.

Germany, Italy, and Japan all wanted more land. Germany began to take over countries in Europe. Italy went to war in Africa. And Japan took large parts of China. The three countries agreed to help each other. They became known as the Axis Powers.

In the 1940s, Franklin Roosevelt was the President of the United States, and Winston Churchill was the leader of Great Britain.

## World War II Begins

In March 1939, Hitler demanded that Poland give Germany some land. Germany had lost this land in World War I. Poland was afraid of Hitler. It asked Great Britain to help if Germany attacked. Great Britain agreed.

In September, Hitler did what people feared. He sent the German Army into Poland. The army moved very quickly and soon took control of Poland. Great Britain and France then announced that they were at war with Germany. World War II had begun.

**Why did Great Britain go to war against Germany?**

The Germans continued to attack other countries. First they took over Denmark and Norway. Then they captured the Netherlands and Belgium. The German Army soon controlled most of France.

Then the Germans began a war in the air against Great Britain. They sent planes to drop bombs on the British night after night.

By 1941, Hitler had captured many European countries. Still, most Americans did not want to join the war. All that President Roosevelt could do was lend ships and guns to Great Britain.

**169**

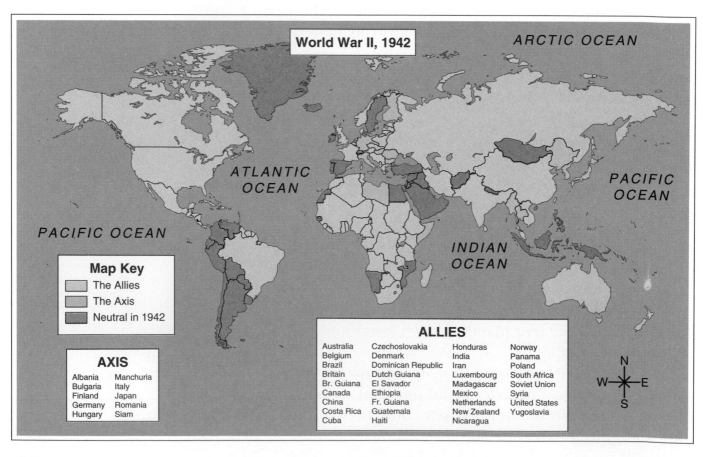

## Americans Join the War

On December 7, 1941, Japanese planes attacked the American Navy at Pearl Harbor, Hawaii. The Japanese were trying to keep the United States out of the war. The Japanese tried to destroy enough ships to keep our navy from fighting. This did not happen. The attack made the United States join the war.

**Why did the Japanese attack Pearl Harbor?**

_____

_____

After the shock of Pearl Harbor, many Americans feared that Japanese Americans might help Japan attack the United States. So Japanese Americans were forced to move to places called **internment camps.** They lost their homes and businesses. Everyone now agrees that this was unfair. The Japanese Americans had done nothing wrong. They were American citizens. In 1988, a law was passed giving $20,000 to each person who spent time in these camps.

This Japanese American family waits to be taken to an internment camp in 1942.

**World War II, 1942**

ARCTIC OCEAN

ATLANTIC OCEAN

PACIFIC OCEAN

PACIFIC OCEAN

INDIAN OCEAN

**Map Key**
- The Allies
- The Axis
- Neutral in 1942

**AXIS**

| | |
|---|---|
| Albania | Manchuria |
| Bulgaria | Italy |
| Finland | Japan |
| Germany | Romania |
| Hungary | Siam |

**ALLIES**

| | | | |
|---|---|---|---|
| Australia | Czechoslovakia | Honduras | Norway |
| Belgium | Denmark | India | Panama |
| Brazil | Dominican Republic | Iran | Poland |
| Britain | Dutch Guiana | Luxembourg | South Africa |
| Br. Guiana | El Savador | Madagascar | Soviet Union |
| Canada | Ethiopia | Mexico | Syria |
| China | Fr. Guiana | Netherlands | United States |
| Costa Rica | Guatemala | New Zealand | Yugoslavia |
| Cuba | Haiti | Nicaragua | |

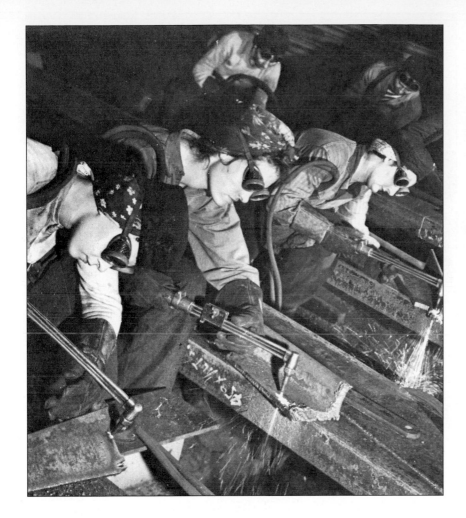

(above) Citizens of a typical American town plant a "victory garden" to help the war effort. (left) During World War II, these women helped make weapons.

The United States joined the Allies in the war. The Allies were Great Britain, the Soviet Union, and other countries that were fighting the Axis powers. Soon millions of Americans had joined the armed forces. They were quickly trained and sent to fight in Africa and in the Pacific Islands.

American factories began making more tanks, guns, and other weapons. Again, as in World War I, women went to work in the factories. Families grew vegetables in their backyards so that farm foods could be sent to the soldiers. Children collected tin cans and other metals needed to make weapons.

**How did Americans help their soldiers in World War II?**

Don't forget to find out about the music that people liked to listen to and dance to during World War II. Find examples that reflected the war. Look for British and American songs.

Allied soldiers land on the coast of France on June 6, 1944.

## War in Europe

The Allies fought first in North Africa, not Europe. They won back the countries that Germany and Italy had taken. Then, in the summer of 1943, they crossed from North Africa to Italy.

The hardest battle of the war was fought on the beaches of France. The Allies had planned it for two years. The Germans knew the British and Americans would try to get to France from Great Britain. The Germans built forts to keep the Allies from landing. But early in the morning of June 6, 1944, the Allies attacked. They came in 2,700 ships. Other soldiers flew across in planes and landed behind the Germans. We call the battle D-Day.

When D-Day was over, the Allies finally had a place to land their troops. In less than a month, there were a million Allied soldiers in France.

But the war was not over yet. The Allied troops won many battles, but the Germans continued to fight. It was almost a year before the Allies finally reached Berlin, the German capital. When they did, Hitler killed himself. After that, the German Army gave up.

**What was the hardest battle of the war?**

_____

# War In the Pacific

After the attack on Pearl Harbor, the United States quickly rebuilt its navy. Then the ships were ready to join the fight. The United States sent ships and planes to the Pacific Ocean to fight the Japanese. It was not easy to fight there. The Japanese had taken over many islands in an area that was much larger than all of Europe. The Americans had to fight a new battle for every island.

Planes could not fly as far or as fast then as they can now. They needed more places to land. Because there were few places to build airfields, planes had to fly from large ships called aircraft carriers. Planes would land on and take off from these ships. Planes attacked the Japanese forces on the islands while American soldiers tried to land on the beaches. The planes also tried to bomb Japanese ships.

 **Why did American forces use aircraft carriers in the Pacific?**

_____

_____

(above) General Douglas MacArthur led the Americans in the Pacific. (below) This painting shows an American aircraft carrier. A Japanese plane attacking the ship has been shot down.

While the Americans were fighting in the Pacific, British, Chinese, Australians, and others were fighting in the region east of India and south of China. This is called Southeast Asia. Slowly, the Japanese Army lost the islands and countries they had captured.

## The Atomic Bomb

In April 1945, President Roosevelt died. Vice President Harry S. Truman became President. Truman knew that the war in Europe would end soon. But the war in the Pacific might go on for a long time. The Japanese would not give up.

In July 1945, the United States tested an **atomic bomb.** An atomic bomb is many times more powerful than an ordinary bomb. Truman decided to use this bomb to force the Japanese to give up. On August 6, 1945, an American plane dropped an atomic bomb on the city of Hiroshima, Japan. Almost 100,000 people were killed. But the fighting still did not stop. Three days later another American bomb destroyed the city of Nagasaki. World War II was finally over.

(above) President Truman decided to drop the atomic bomb. (below) This is a photograph of Hiroshima, Japan, after the United States dropped the atomic bomb.

 **Why did President Truman decide to use the atomic bomb in Japan?**

As World War II ended, people around the world began to think about peace. Above all, they wondered how they could keep more wars from happening.

In April 1945 there was a meeting in San Francisco, California. People from around the world met to talk about peace. Fifty nations decided to form an organization called the United Nations. You may have heard it called the U.N.

The U.N. built its **headquarters**, or main offices, in New York City. The main job there is to work for peace. People from more than 190 nations meet to talk about problems. Each nation has a chance to tell the others about things that are wrong. The nations try to solve problems by talking, not by wars.

Sometimes the U.N. sends armed forces to try to keep people from fighting. In the 1990s U.N. peacekeepers went to Somalia and Liberia in Africa, Bosnia in Europe, and Haiti.

Former President Bill Clinton addressed the United Nations several times.

The United Nations has other jobs. For example, the U.N. teaches people in poor nations how to farm. It also supplies food to countries that cannot grow enough food.

There are many other parts to the United Nations. Have you ever bought a greeting card from UNICEF? That money helps children all around the world. The World Health Organization sends medicine and doctors to people who need help for medical problems.

The United Nations is not always successful. Some of its member nations have stopped talking and gone to war. But others have solved their problems by talking. If the United Nations did not exist, there might have been more wars.

**How do you think nations would work out their problems if there were no United Nations?**

_____

_____

# CHAPTER ✓ CHECKUP

**Complete each sentence. Circle the letter in front of the correct answer.**

1. The name of the German dictator was
   a. Winston Churchill.
   b. Adolf Hitler.
   c. Franklin Roosevelt.
   d. Benito Mussolini.

2. The Axis Powers included
   a. Germany and Japan.
   b. the United States and Great Britain.
   c. France and the Soviet Union.
   d. all of Europe.

3. The United States entered World War II because
   a. Japan bombed the United States Navy.
   b. Hitler put people in concentration camps.
   c. Germany bombed Great Britain.
   d. it was one of the Allies.

4. D-Day was a battle on the beaches of
   a. Italy.
   b. Japan.
   c. Germany.
   d. France.

5. World War II ended in
   a. 1941.
   b. 1943.
   c. 1944.
   d. 1945.

6. The war in the Pacific ended because
   a. aircraft carriers attacked the islands.
   b. atomic bombs were dropped on Japan.
   c. Adolf Hitler died.
   d. Harry S. Truman was President.

**THINKING AND WRITING**

Why do people today try to remember the Holocaust?

_____

_____

_____

_____

_____

_____

_____

_____

# CHAPTER 17

# America: A Superpower, 1945–Today

After World War II, everyone hoped for more peaceful times. But conflicts still happened.

The two strongest nations after the war were the United States and the Soviet Union. These two powerful nations were called superpowers.

This chapter tells how the superpowers stopped being allies. For nearly 50 years, they were enemies in what was called the **Cold War**. Enemies in a cold war fight with words and ideas instead of guns.

You will find out how the Cold War developed into "hot wars" in Korea and Vietnam. Later, the chapter tells what happened to the Soviet Union and describes the world today.

Even though the Cold War ended, wars still happened. The United States was attacked, and it was involved in three conflicts in the Middle East.

**What happened between the two superpowers after World War II?**

Moscow was the capital of the Soviet Union. Today it is the capital of Russia.

This man votes in an election in Texas. Voting is an important right in democratic countries like the United States.

## Two Countries

The United States and the Soviet Union each thought it had a better kind of government. The Soviet Union had a kind of government called **communism.** The Communists believed that the workers, not people with money, should own businesses, factories, and land. The workers should receive all the money from the work they do.

At first, the Soviet government followed this idea. Later, the government took control of factories and land away from workers. The communist government also did not allow the people to choose who would govern them. It did not allow anyone to argue with the government or try to change it.

In the United States, people may own businesses, factories, and farms and make money from them. They can also make money by buying and selling shares of stock in businesses. The government does not own these things. People in this country are also free to choose who will govern them. They can argue with the government as long as they do not break the laws. This makes our government a democracy.

The Soviet Union wanted other countries to be communist. Americans believed democracy was better than communism. Americans wanted to keep other nations from becoming communist.

 **Name one way the government of the Soviet Union differed from the government of the United States.**

## A Divided Germany

After the war, the Soviet Union took control of many countries. These included Poland, Lithuania, Romania, and Czechoslovakia. Soviet leaders wanted to spread communism to the countries near Russia.

The Soviet Union already controlled part of Germany. After the war, Germany had been divided into four parts.

 **Look at the map below. What countries governed the other three parts of Germany?**

_____

_____

The city of Berlin was divided in the same way. Berlin was inside the Soviet part of Germany. In 1948, the Soviets decided they wanted all of Berlin. They blocked all roads leading to the city. No food or supplies could get into the city. The Soviets hoped to force the other countries out of Berlin.

But the United States did not give in. It sent planes with food and supplies to the people of Berlin. After 11 months, the Soviets took down the roadblocks.

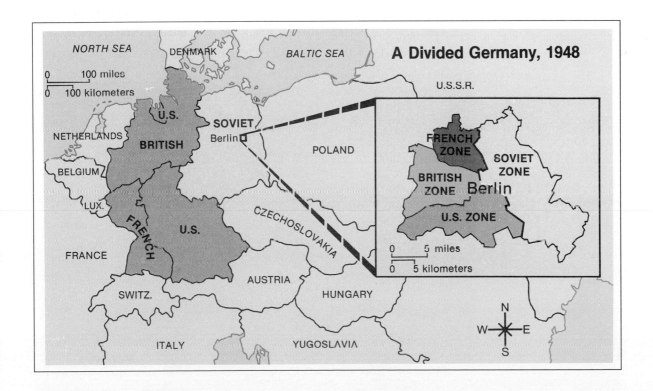

A Divided Germany, 1948

The three parts of western Germany became one country in 1955. West Germany had a democratic government. The same year, the Soviet Union let East Germany become a separate nation. But East Germany had a communist government.

In 1961, the Communists built a wall across Berlin. It divided communist East Berlin from West Berlin. It was built to keep people from leaving communist countries in eastern Europe.

## The War in Korea

In some parts of Asia, the Cold War became "hot." After World War II, Korea was divided into two parts: North Korea and South Korea. In 1950, communist North Korea tried to take over South Korea. Another communist country, China, sent troops to help the North Koreans. The United Nations decided to send troops to help South Korea. There were many American soldiers among the U.N. troops.

 **Look at the map. Why was it easy for China to help North Korea?**

In 1952, Dwight D. Eisenhower became President of the United States. He helped end the Korean War in July 1953. Over three million civilians and soldiers from both sides had been killed. Today, North Korea and South Korea are still separate countries.

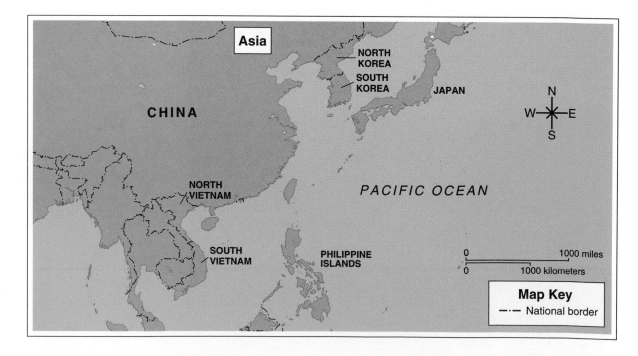

180

# The War in Vietnam

In the 1960s, another war began in Asia. This war was in Vietnam. Before World War II, Vietnam was a French colony. Later, it was divided into two countries called North Vietnam and South Vietnam.

The government of North Vietnam was communist. The North Vietnamese wanted to take over South Vietnam. But the leaders of South Vietnam did not want their country to be communist. Not everyone in South Vietnam agreed with these leaders. They began to fight against their government. North Vietnam helped these South Vietnamese Communists, who were called the Viet Cong.

**Who were the Viet Cong?**

These U.S. soldiers regroup in a Vietnam jungle.

The United States supported the South Vietnamese government. Our government was afraid that if South Vietnam became communist, all of Asia would become communist.

The United States sent soldiers to fight the Viet Cong and to keep the North Vietnamese out of South Vietnam. It was a difficult war. The Viet Cong knew the land. They knew how to hide and fight in the jungle. Many battles were fought in rice fields and farms. Many farmers and their families died in the war, as well as soldiers on both sides.

In the United States, thousands of people **protested,** or spoke out against, the war. They marched, sang, and made speeches against the war. They said the United States had nothing to gain from the war.

Finally, in March 1973, American soldiers left Vietnam. They had not defeated the Communists. Two years later, North Vietnam and South Vietnam were joined together under communist rule.

**UNIT PROJECT Tip**

Learn something about songs such as "Blowin' in the Wind," "Universal Soldier," "Sky Pilot," and "The Ballad of the Green Berets" that became popular during the time of the Vietnam War.

# The Arms Race

Part of the Cold War was called the arms race. The United States and the Soviet Union each tried to be the first to build new **arms,** or weapons. Many were very powerful weapons, like the atomic bomb.

Neither country wanted to use these weapons. But each side wanted to have more weapons than the other side. Some Americans said that the United States should spend less on guns, bombs, and planes. Others felt that if each side had the same number of weapons, neither side would go to war.

In 1963, the United States, the Soviet Union, and Great Britain agreed to stop testing weapons. Over the following years, the United States and the Soviet Union agreed to make fewer powerful weapons.

The Strategic Arms Reduction Talks (START) began in 1982. In 1991, President George Bush and Soviet leader Mikhail Gorbachev signed the START I Treaty. In it, the United States and the Soviet Union agreed to destroy many atomic weapons.

**What was important about the START I Treaty?**

_____

_____

In 1987, Soviet leader Mikhail Gorbachev and President Ronald Reagan signed a treaty to make fewer powerful weapons. The treaty helped set the stage for the signing of the START I Treaty.

# The End of the Soviet Union

After many years, the Cold War began to slow down. Soviet leader Mikhail Gorbachev tried to be friendlier to the United States.

The Soviet Union itself started to change. Gorbachev knew that his country had many problems. It could not make enough goods or grow enough food for its people. Soviet people had to stand in line for hours to buy shoes or to buy food.

But the Soviet people wanted more than food and clothes. They were unhappy because they could not vote or speak out. They wanted freedom. Gorbachev agreed that there should be more freedom in communist countries. He decided to ask western countries for help. He met with President Reagan and later with President Bush.

In the late 1980s, many people in communist countries like Poland and East Germany said they did not want to be controlled by the Soviets. They wanted a choice in their government. The communist governments had to listen. In 1989, East Germany's government took down the Berlin Wall.

The Soviet Union had been made up of Russia and other regions called republics. Russia and the republics in the Soviet Union had one government. Now these republics wanted more control over themselves. Gorbachev and the leaders of some republics signed a treaty in 1991. It gave the republics more freedom from the Soviet government.

This worried other Soviet leaders. They were afraid Gorbachev and others were destroying communism and the Soviet Union. They tried to stop him, but they failed. The Communists lost all their power in the government. In December of 1991, the Soviet Union broke up into separate nations. Boris Yeltsin became the leader of the strongest of the new nations, Russia.

(top) President Ronald Reagan and Vice President George Bush. (bottom) Russian president Boris Yeltsin.

**What happened in the communist countries during the late 1980s and early 1990s?**

_____

_____

183

## A Changing World

The years following 1991 were hard for Russia and some of the countries that once had communist governments. They found it slow and difficult to change from communism to democracy. Some areas that are part of Russia want to be separate countries.

Elections have been held in the new nations that were once part of the Soviet Union. Slowly things are getting better in these countries. For example, in 1995, factory production started to grow in Russia after falling for four years.

## The Persian Gulf War

In 1991, the United States went to war again. In 1990, Iraq took over the tiny country of Kuwait. Kuwait is near the Persian Gulf. Iraq wanted Kuwait's oil. The United States was afraid that Iraq would try to take over other countries in that region. If Iraq did this, it would control most of the oil in the world.

The United States sent troops to the neighboring country of Saudi Arabia. In January 1991, the United States, with help from other countries, sent planes to bomb Iraq's capital. Then troops went into Iraq and Kuwait. In just a few days the troops freed Kuwait and the war ended.

 **Look at the map. What body of water is next to Kuwait?**

_____

U.S. troops check their equipment after arriving at an air base in Saudi Arabia in 1990.

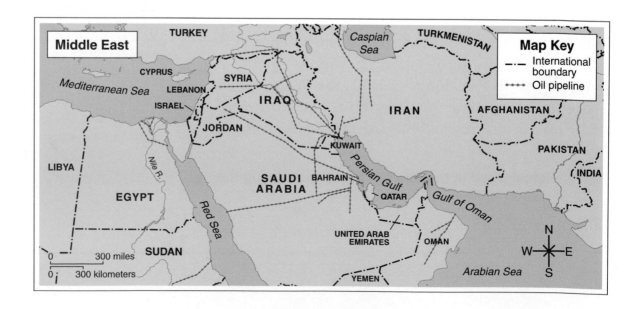

**184**

## The United States Is Attacked

In the late 1980s or early 1990s, a man from Saudi Arabia named Osama bin Laden founded an organization called Al Qaeda, which is an Arabic word meaning "the Base."

Al Qaeda may have been created to support Muslims who were fighting the Soviet Union in Afghanistan. Later, in the 1990s, Osama bin Laden and Al Qaeda said they were at war with the United States.

Al Qaeda terrorists, people who use violence to cause fear, first attacked the United States in 1993 when they planted a bomb at the World Trade Center in New York. They destroyed U.S. embassies in Kenya and Tanzania, in Africa, in 1998. In 2000, Al Qaeda terrorists attacked a U.S. warship, the *U.S.S. Cole*, in Yemen, also in Africa.

Then, on September 11, 2001, Al Qaeda terrorists used commercial airplanes to attack the World Trade Center in New York City and the Pentagon in Washington, D.C. They killed more than 3,400 people. The two towers of the World Trade Center collapsed.

It took one year and the efforts of some 3,000 people to rebuild the Pentagon, headquarters of the Department of Defense, after the attack.

## The World Today

The United States and its allies have declared a "war on terror" throughout the world. Because Al Qaeda had its headquarters in Afghanistan, troops from the United States and its allies invaded and occupied Afghanistan in late 2001.

In 2003, the United States and its allies again went to war against Iraq and occupied that country.

In the 2004 U.S. elections, George W. Bush won a second term as President. He told voters he would continue fighting terrorists throughout the world.

**What is the greatest threat facing the United States today?**

_____

_____

President George W. Bush

185

# The Peace Corps

In this chapter, you've been reading about a lot of problems between countries around the world. Many people have tried to find ways to solve these problems. One thing some Americans tried was the Peace Corps.

In 1961, a new President took office. His name was John F. Kennedy. Kennedy was young and full of energy. He and some other people came up with the idea of the Peace Corps. Kennedy said the Peace Corps would send Americans to help people in other parts of the world help themselves.

Americans who joined the Peace Corps were sent to nations all over the world. People in these nations learned many skills from Peace Corps teachers. They learned how to build houses. They learned better ways to farm and how to start small factories. They learned better ways to keep people healthy and care for the sick.

Today, Peace Corps members are still trying to help people improve their lives in Africa, Asia, Eastern Europe, and Latin America.

**If you could teach something, what would it be? What skills would you like to learn?**

In Togo, a small country in western Africa, a Peace Corps volunteer nurse and a Togolese assistant check the weights and general health of babies in a village. They also distribute health-care information.

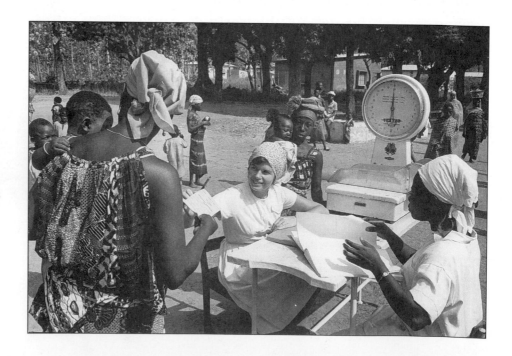

**Complete each sentence. Circle the letter in front of the correct answer.**

1. A Cold War is fought
   a. with weapons.
   b. with many soldiers.
   c. with words and ideas.
   d. in the winter.

2. After World War II, the Soviet Union
   a. took over many countries.
   b. fought in the Vietnam War.
   c. did what the United States wanted.
   d. gave its part of Germany to the United Nations.

3. The United States fought the Vietnam War because it did not want Vietnam to be
   a. democratic
   b. communist.
   c. rich.
   d. in the United Nations.

4. In the START I Treaty, the United States and the Soviet Union agreed to
   a. join the United Nations.
   b. fight Iraq.
   c. destroy some of their weapons.
   d. elect a President.

5. The Soviet leader who made changes that helped end the Soviet Union was
   a. George Bush.
   b. Mikhail Gorbachev.
   c. Ronald Reagan.
   d. Boris Yeltsin.

6. Iraq took over Kuwait because it wanted Kuwait's
   a. gold.
   b. water.
   c. airplanes.
   d. oil.

**THINKING AND WRITING**

What are some ways the world has changed since the end of World War II?

_____

_____

_____

_____

_____

_____

_____

_____

# New Hopes, New Dreams, 1945–Today

On July 20, 1969, American astronauts were the first to land on the moon. After World War II, the United States space program used computers to control equipment and track information. Soon the Space Age turned into the Information Age.

 **The astronauts put the American flag on the moon. Why do you think they did this?**

Americans were interested in other things, too. People were worried about protecting Earth. Others were working for equal rights for all Americans. This has been an age of new hopes and new dreams for the United States. Of course, it has been an age of great change.

An American astronaut during the Apollo 11 mission, the first mission to land astronauts on the moon.

## Keeping Dreams Alive

Americans did well and looked toward the future with hope after World War II. But in the 1960s our hopes and dreams were almost crushed.

President John Kennedy wanted equal rights for all Americans. He promised that the United States would move ahead of the Soviet Union in space. Then, in 1963, a man named Lee Harvey Oswald **assassinated,** or murdered, President Kennedy. Two other leaders, President Kennedy's brother, Robert, and African American leader Dr. Martin Luther King, Jr., were also assassinated during the 1960s. Americans were very sad. They feared violence would destroy the nation.

Then there was the Vietnam War. Many people were strongly against the war. Others were not. Before the war ended, it almost tore the nation apart.

Little by little, the United States recovered. Hopes and dreams returned and helped Americans move beyond the bad times. Many people gained their civil rights. American science kept changing our lives.

## Equal Justice for All

Even after World War II, laws in the South kept African Americans **segregated,** or apart, from whites. African Americans could not go to the same schools or restaurants as white Americans. In the North, there were no laws to segregate the African Americans. Most still could not go to good schools or get good jobs.

**Civil rights** are those rights that make it possible for everyone to be treated equally. Many people spoke out about how unfair it was that African Americans did not have civil rights. African Americans and other Americans began working to make sure all people were treated equally under our laws.

(top) Lyndon Johnson became President after Kennedy's death. He helped make Kennedy's ideas into laws. (bottom) Rosa Parks protested the segregation of African Americans from white Americans on buses in Montgomery, Alabama. Here she sits in a seat of her choice.

**What was unfair about the laws that segregated people in the South?**

UNIT PROJECT Tip

What kind of music became most popular in the 1960s? How did it seem to reflect the times?

## Winning Civil Rights

In 1951, Linda Brown wanted to go to a public high school near her home in Topeka, Kansas. Linda was African American, and the school was for white Americans only. Linda's father felt this was wrong. He went to court to have it changed.

Finally, in 1954, Mr. Brown's case reached the Supreme Court. The court said it was against the Constitution to have separate schools for white Americans and African Americans. No American school could be segregated. The Browns had won an important civil right in the courts.

In Montgomery, Alabama, and other southern cities, African Americans had to ride in the back of buses. Civil rights leaders like Dr. Martin Luther King, Jr., told them not to ride those buses until they could sit where they wanted. They stayed off the buses for over a year. The bus companies lost so much money that they finally gave in. After that, African Americans had the right to sit anywhere on the city's buses.

**What did African Americans do to win civil rights? List two things they did.**

(top) These disabled Americans protest for equal rights. Many new laws have been passed in recent years to assist disabled Americans. (bottom) Hundreds of thousands of African Americans traveled from across the country in 1995 to promote racial unity by participating in the Million Man March in Washington, D.C.

People fought for civil rights for many years. Finally, Congress passed the Civil Rights Act of 1964. This law said that businesses like hotels and restaurants had to serve everyone. It also stated that it was against the law to refuse people a job because of their race, religion, sex, or national background.

In later years, more Americans have used votes, the courts, and protests to win their civil rights. For example, Hispanics and American Indians are trying to change what is unfair to them. Women of all backgrounds still work to gain the same rights as men. Disabled Americans are asking to be treated equally. Things are better today than they were forty years ago. But the struggle for civil rights still goes on.

# The Space Age

In 1957, the Soviet Union sent the first **satellite** into space. A satellite is a machine that is sent into space, miles above Earth. Satellites are still used for sending television communications around the world. Others help study the weather or spy on other countries.

Americans landed on the moon in July 1969 and brought back much information. Today, we learn about space in other ways. Planetary probes are spacecraft that carry cameras and other instruments instead of people. Probes have told us a great many new facts about the planets in our solar system.

**Space shuttles** carry people. A space shuttle looks a little like a plane and can be used again and again. Scientists on the shuttles study the weather and space. They have tried to find out what it is like to live in space. In 1995, for the first time, an American shuttle met an orbiting space station from Russia. There have been many meetings since.

**What are three kinds of spacecraft?**

_____

_____

In 1990, the United States sent the Hubble Space Telescope into orbit. There were some problems with it at first, but once corrected, it began to send in very clear pictures of outer space to Earth. The Hubble Telescope marked a new beginning of discoveries about space.

(above) This photograph of a space probe was made by a computer. It shows how space probes observe floating objects, temperature, radiation, and other conditions while exploring far into space. (left) Astronauts from the United States, Russia, and other nations built an international space station. This was one model of the future space station.

**191**

# The Information Age

The United States changed quickly in the second half of the 1900s. Television and the computer had a lot to do with those changes.

Television changed America's way of thinking. Suddenly, Americans could see the news as it was happening. Television became part of elections. Even wars came into American homes.

The first computer was as big as a room and could not do very much. But by the 1980s, computers were much smaller and more powerful. Scientists used computers. Most businesses used them.

Today, computers are everywhere. In stores, school classrooms, and homes, people are solving problems with computers. They are learning things, playing games, and keeping track of information. Many people carry around computers the size of a large book.

Computers can be connected to one another by telephone lines. This means that people can use computers to communicate with each other around the world. They can get information stored in libraries in faraway states and even countries. People can communicate with one another by computer. They even can shop. And they can do this without leaving their homes and offices!

**What are three ways that people use computers in their homes?**

(above) Some laptop computers are small enough to take along on a sailboat. (right) ENIAC was the first computer. It was built in 1946. It was used mainly to solve math problems.

## Problems Come with Successes

The United States has had more successes than any other nation in the world. It is still rich and free. Americans hope that the country can keep growing and solving its problems in the 2000s as it did in the 1900s. The problems facing America today include finding better ways to make energy and protecting the environment. They include making sure everyone has a job that pays enough money to live, and finding ways to remain free while stopping violence and terrorists.

## Better Ways to Make Energy

The United States uses more oil than any other nation. We use oil to make electricity and to make gasoline and plastics. There is not enough oil in the United States for our needs. We have to import oil from other nations.

In the 1970s, oil was hard to get. Americans worried about having enough. They spent hours in lines at gas stations, hoping there would be some gas left when it was their turn. This was an energy crisis. People learned that they had to **conserve,** or save, oil through careful use.

 **Many cars today use less gasoline. How is this a way to conserve oil?**

(above) A wind machine is one of many new ways to make energy. (below) During the energy crisis, people waited in long lines to buy gas.

8-GALLON LIMIT, PLEASE

TO SERVE ALL OUR CUSTOMERS, WE MUST LIMIT INDIVIDUAL GASOLINE PURCHASES. YOUR COOPERATION IS APPRECIATED.

193

Not too far in the future, Earth's oil will be used up. So the United States and other nations are trying to find new ways to make electricity and to run cars. For example, the atomic power that makes bombs can also be used to make electricity. Many people think this is dangerous, though. The sun's power can be also used to make electricity—and even make cars run. But we need to find better ways to do it. If we can, we may be able to prevent an energy crisis in the future.

## Protecting the Environment

Using oil for energy is one thing that causes **pollution,** or dirt in the environment. The **environment** is made up of the air, land, oceans, lakes, and rivers. People realize that pollution is very bad. It can kill fish, plants, animals, and even people. Today, Americans see that they need to protect the environment.

Many things cause pollution besides using oil. Many factories pollute air and water with chemicals they use to make goods. People pollute when they throw their trash away. Garbage is a big problem. We are running out of places to put garbage. Burning garbage is not a good solution, because it causes air pollution.

We must learn to **recycle,** or use things again. Glass, paper, and aluminum cans can be recycled. This also means that we do not need more energy to make new glass, paper, or cans. Many Americans are trying to get more laws to protect our air, water, and land.

 **What are some ways we can protect the environment?**

_____

_____

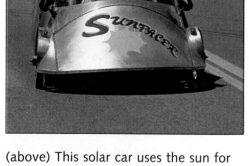

(above) This solar car uses the sun for energy. When the car runs, it does not cause pollution. (right) These teens are helping to clean up Town Lake in Austin, Texas.

## Making Money to Live

After World War II, people were making more money. Prices often rose, but so did wages. One working person could usually make enough for a family to live. Employers helped pay for workers' health care.

Slowly, in the 1980s, things began to change. Businesses and other groups needed fewer workers. People lost jobs. Employers gave less money for workers' health care. Wages grew more slowly. There were fewer ways for workers to move up to better-paying jobs in their companies.

Today, often two people must hold jobs to make enough money for one family. Even though many businesses are making more money, workers' wages have not grown much. Americans are finding they must be more careful with their money.

**Why are things harder for workers today?**

The Alfred P. Murrah Federal Building in Oklahoma City was the target of a bomb attack on April 19, 1995.

## Stopping Violence

Another problem that needs to be solved in the United States is violence. Some people use violence to steal money or get drugs. People often do not talk through their problems. Instead, they use fists, guns, and other weapons to get their own way. They even try to settle small arguments in a violent way.

Like terrorists from other countries, a few Americans believe that government is their enemy. Some are willing to use violence against the government. In 1995, a government building in Oklahoma City was blown up. In the blast, 168 men, women, and children were killed. It was the work of Americans, not foreign enemies.

How will Americans solve such problems? No one knows for sure. But we have overcome problems before. We must hope that we can use new knowledge, hard work, and a lot of care to do so again.

Dr. Martin Luther King, Jr.

When the African Americans of Montgomery, Alabama, met about segregation on the buses, they were angry. Yet they protested in a peaceful way. Why?

The leader of the meeting was a young man named Dr. Martin Luther King, Jr. He did not believe in using violence. Instead he used **nonviolence.** He felt that people should work together peacefully to gain their rights. They should not fight back if they were attacked. Dr. King was sure that nonviolence was right. He urged people to protest peacefully, even when it was difficult and dangerous.

In 1963, Dr. King led a huge march on Washington, D.C., to show support for civil rights. People all over the world respected him as a leader who won civil rights.

On April 4, 1968, Dr. King was shot and killed in Memphis, Tennessee. People were very angry. Some people said nonviolence had failed. But other people have gone on doing things Dr. King's way. They wanted to continue Dr. King's dream for a better life for all people.

Since Dr. King's death, African Americans have made progress. They have won places in American businesses, universities, and government. African Americans serve in the United States Congress, as well as on the Supreme Court.

Dr. Martin Luther King, Jr., is a model for our nation's leaders. He not only thought of new solutions to problems. He also knew how to get people to agree to those solutions without violence.

**Why did people respect Dr. Martin Luther King, Jr.?**

_____

_____

# CHAPTER ✓ CHECKUP

**Complete each sentence. Circle the letter in front of the correct answer.**

1. John F. Kennedy and Dr. Martin Luther King, Jr., were both
   a. elected President of the United States.
   b. assassinated.
   c. astronauts.
   d. African Americans.

2. Civil rights are the rights of all citizens to
   a. make a living.
   b. use computers to communicate.
   c. be treated equally.
   d. be segregated.

3. Voting, marches, and using the courts are ways to
   a. change unfair laws.
   b. get people to like you.
   c. win elections.
   d. use computers.

4. Computers help people
   a. do the laundry and other household chores.
   b. see the news as it happens.
   c. solve problems and learn things.
   d. save electricity.

5. Pollution is a problem because it
   a. needs oil.
   b. causes an energy crisis.
   c. can never be changed.
   d. damages our environment.

6. In the United States, violence
   a. is a problem we have solved.
   b. is something people sometimes use to solve their problems.
   c. is a problem we will never solve.
   d. has never been a problem.

**THINKING AND WRITING** What do you think would have happened if Dr. Martin Luther King, Jr., had not been assassinated?

_____

_____

_____

_____

_____

_____

# Using a Map with an Inset

Look at the map and the inset below to find out more about the battles of World War II that were fought in Asia and the Pacific.

1. Which map would you use to find out the date of the Japanese attack on Pearl Harbor?

   _____

2. Did the Japanese gain or lose territory after the attack on Pearl Harbor?

   _____

3. Who held the Philippines by the end of 1942?

   _____

4. Is the island of Oahu bigger or smaller than Taiwan?

   _____

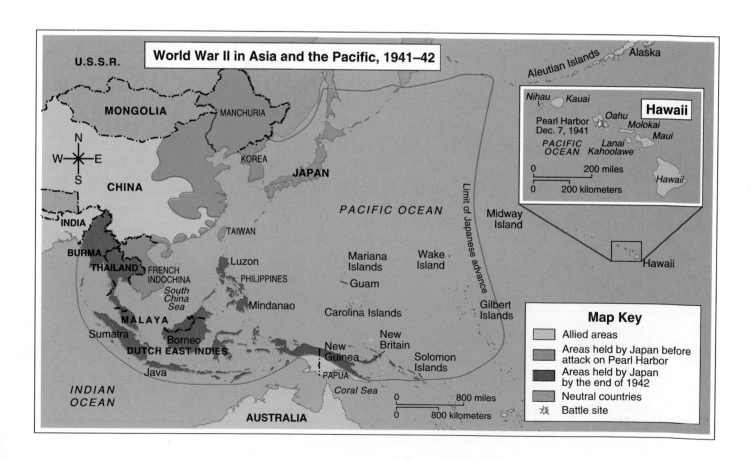

Now it is time to finish your unit project. Think about all the popular music you have learned about. Talk with your team about answers to questions like these.

- **What kinds of music have been popular in the United States from the 1920s to the present?**

- **How was the music created and how did it become popular?**

- **How did popular music reflect the times?**

Decide how you want to present your project. Choose one of these ways or use one of your own ideas.

➤ Tape a collection of examples of the music you studied. Write a narration to announce and explain each example. Have team members take turns reading and taping the narration. Play the narrated tape for other teams.

➤ Present a live musical show. Have team members perform selections of the music you studied. Some students may want to play or sing their selections. Others can mime or "lip-sync" to recorded selections. You might wear costumes. One person can announce each number. Put on your show for an audience of other teams or classes—or for your families.

➤ Make a musical time line mural for the wall of your classroom. Different team members can be responsible for each time period. Write the names of songs and some of the lyrics you like on colored paper. Place them on the time line. Add pictures of people and events that go along with the songs.

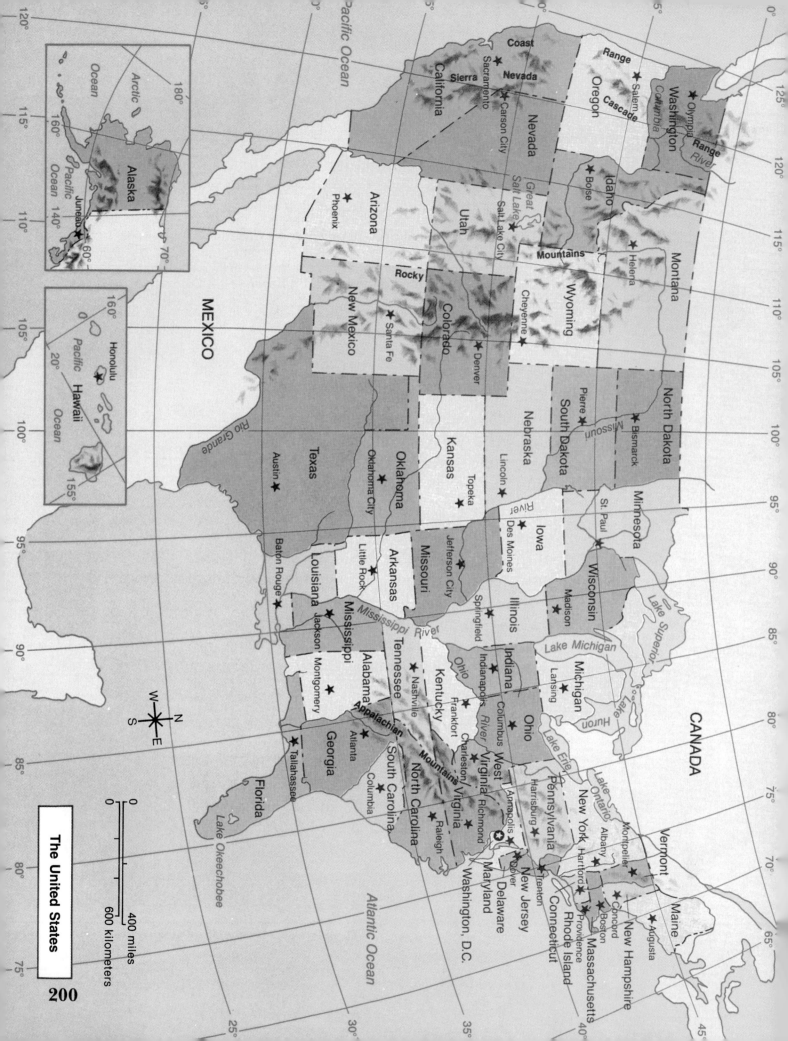

# The United States

200

0
400 miles
0
600 kilometers

**Inset (top left):**
Arctic Ocean
Pacific Ocean
Alaska
Juneau
180°
160°
140°
70°
60°

**Inset (left):**
Pacific Ocean
Hawaii
Honolulu
160°
155°
20°

MEXICO

CANADA

Pacific Ocean

Atlantic Ocean

**States and features:**

Washington — Olympia
Coast Range
Cascade Range
Columbia River
Oregon — Salem
California — Sacramento
Sierra Nevada
Carson City
Nevada
Idaho — Boise
Montana — Helena
Great Salt Lake
Salt Lake City
Utah
Arizona — Phoenix
Rocky Mountains
New Mexico — Santa Fe
Colorado — Denver
Wyoming — Cheyenne
North Dakota — Bismarck
South Dakota — Pierre
Missouri River
Nebraska — Lincoln
Kansas — Topeka
Oklahoma — Oklahoma City
Texas — Austin
Rio Grande
Minnesota — St. Paul
Iowa — Des Moines
Wisconsin — Madison
Lake Superior
Michigan — Lansing
Lake Michigan
Lake Huron
Illinois — Springfield
Indiana — Indianapolis
Ohio — Columbus
Ohio River
Lake Erie
Lake Ontario
Missouri — Jefferson City
Arkansas — Little Rock
Louisiana — Baton Rouge
Mississippi River
Mississippi — Jackson
Alabama — Montgomery
Tennessee — Nashville
Kentucky — Frankfort
West Virginia — Charleston
Virginia — Richmond
Appalachian Mountains
North Carolina — Raleigh
South Carolina — Columbia
Georgia — Atlanta
Florida — Tallahassee
Lake Okeechobee
Maryland — Annapolis
Washington, D.C.
Delaware — Dover
New Jersey — Trenton
Pennsylvania — Harrisburg
New York — Albany
Connecticut — Hartford
Rhode Island — Providence
Massachusetts — Boston
Vermont — Montpelier
New Hampshire — Concord
Maine — Augusta

Compass rose: N, S, E, W

Longitude/latitude lines: 125°, 120°, 115°, 110°, 105°, 100°, 95°, 90°, 85°, 80°, 75°, 70°, 65°, 45°, 40°, 35°, 30°, 25°

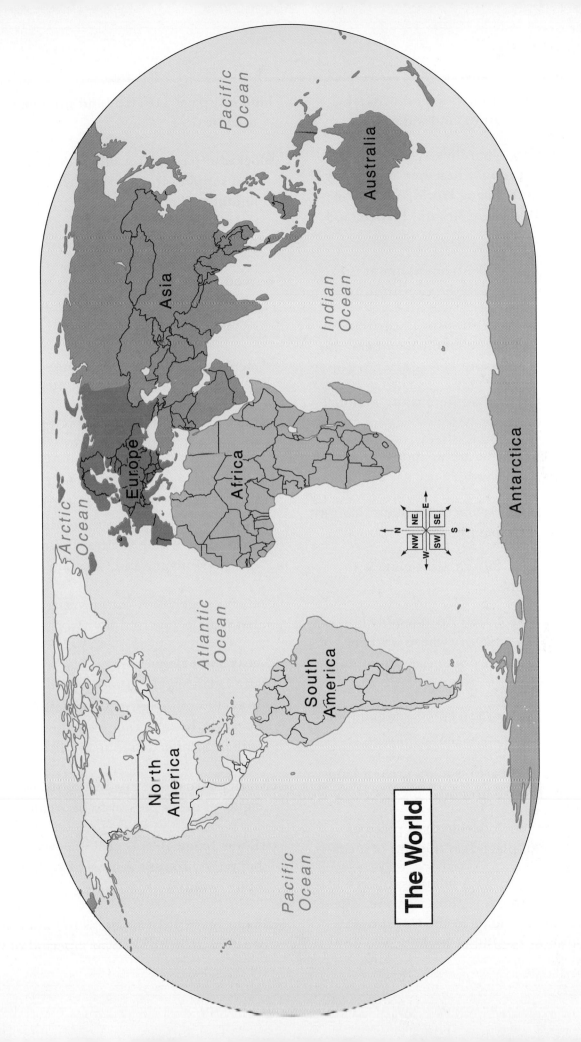

The World

# Glossary

**adobe** (page 11) Adobe is a kind of brick made from clay, straw, and water.

**Allies** (page 149) The Allies were a group of countries that fought together against the Central Powers during World War I. The Allies included Great Britain, France, and Russia.

**amendment** (page 71) An amendment is a change or addition to the Constitution.

**ancestor** (page 7) An ancestor is a parent, grandparent, and the family members who came before a person.

**anthem** (page 81) An anthem is the national song of a country.

**arms** (page 182) Arms are weapons, such as guns, knives, or bombs.

**artifacts** (page 13) Artifacts are items that give clues about how people lived.

**assassinate** (page 189) To assassinate is to murder someone.

**assembly line** (page 159) An assembly line is a moving belt in a factory where workers make something by doing the same thing over and over.

**atomic bomb** (page 174) An atomic bomb is a very powerful weapon that explodes.

**basin** (page 10) A basin is a low area of land with high sides all around.

**bayonet** (page 60) A bayonet is a piece of pointed metal placed on the end of a rifle.

**bill of rights** (page 71) A bill of rights is a list of rights and freedoms for everyone. The first ten amendments to the Constitution are known as the Bill of Rights.

**bind up** (page 116) To bind up means to close.

**blockade** (page 80) A blockade keeps people and supplies from getting from one place to another. The North put ships along the coast to make a blockade against the South during the Civil War.

**boycott** (page 46) To boycott is to stop buying goods in order to make someone do something.

**burgess** (page 27) A burgess was a man chosen to make laws for all the colonists.

**cavalry** (page 146) A cavalry is a group of soldiers who fight on horses.

**Central Powers** (page 149) The Central Powers were a group of countries that fought together against the Allies during World War I. The Central Powers included Austria-Hungary and Germany.

**century** (page 20) A century is a period of 100 years.

**checks and balances** (page 71) With checks and balances, the power of the three branches of the government is limited, or checked, by the other branches. The power is then balanced among all three branches.

**civil rights** (page 189) Civil rights are the rights of every person to be treated equally.

**civil war** (page 109) A civil war is a fight between different groups of people in the same country.

**climate** (page 10) Climate is the kind of weather an area has over a period of time.

**cold war** (page 177) A cold war is a war fought with words and ideas instead of guns. The Cold War was between the United States and the Soviet Union.

**colonist** (page 25) A colonist is a person who lives in a country ruled by another nation.

**colony** (page 25) A colony is a settlement in one country that is ruled by the government of another country.

**commander** (page 50) A commander is a leader. George Washington was the commander of the first American Army.

**common** (page 82) A common person is an ordinary person, not royalty.

**communism** (page 178) Communism is a kind of government in which people do not have the freedom to choose how they want to live.

**compact** (page 29) A compact is a written agreement or promise.

**compromise** (page 69) To compromise means that each side gives in a little in order to reach an understanding.

**concentration camp** (page 168) A concentration camp is a kind of prison.

**congress** (page 67) A congress is a group of people who make a nation's laws.

**conserve** (page 193) To conserve something is to save it through careful use.

**constitution** (page 68) A constitution is a group of laws.

**cowboy** (page 141) A cowboy is a person who works on a ranch.

**culture** (page 8) A culture is a way of living shared by a group of people.

**defeat** (page 111) A defeat is a loss.

**delegate** (page 68) A delegate is a person chosen to represent other people.

**democracy** (page 27) A democracy is a kind of government. In a democracy all people have the same rights and can choose their own leaders.

**democratic** (page 82) A democratic nation treats people as equals.

**depression** (page 162) A depression is a time when there is not enough money or work.

**dictator** (page 167) A dictator is someone who has complete control of a country.

**earth lodge** (page 11) An earth lodge is a round house built with dirt and dried plants. Earth lodges were used by some groups of American Indians.

**empire** (page 19) An empire is a group of lands under one ruler.

**environment** (page 194) The environment is the air, water, and land around us.

**explorer** (page 17) An explorer is a person who travels where no one has ever been before.

**federal system** (page 70) A federal system is a kind of government in which states and cities share power with the national government.

**forty-niner** (page 90) A forty-niner was a person who went to California to look for gold during the Gold Rush of 1849.

**free state** (page 104) Before the Civil War, a free state was a state that did not allow slavery.

**frontier** (page 41) A frontier is the farthest edge of a country, where few people live.

**glaciers** (page 6) Glaciers are large sheets of ice that cover land.

**headquarters** (page 175) Headquarters are main offices. The headquarters of the United Nations is in New York City.

**Holocaust** (page 168) The Holocaust was the mass murder of six million Jews by the German Nazis in the 1930s.

**homesteader** (page 139) A homesteader is a person who lives and farms on land given to that person by the government.

**immigrant** (page 126) An immigrant is a person who leaves one country to live in another country.

**import** (page 46) To import is to bring something from one country into another country.

**independence** (page 44) Independence is freedom from the control of others.

**internment camps** (page 170) Internment camps are places where Japanese Americans were forced to move during World War II.

**labor union** (page 130) A labor union is a group of workers who join together to protect their jobs and to improve working conditions.

**legislature** (page 30) A legislature is a group of people who make laws.

**longhouse** (page 12) A longhouse is a long wooden house with a curved roof. This is the kind of house used by some American Indian groups.

**loyal** (page 55) A loyal person is someone who is faithful.

**Loyalist** (page 55) A Loyalist was a person who was on the side of Great Britain during the American Revolution.

**neutral** (page 149) A neutral country does not enter a war.

**nonviolence** (page 196) Nonviolence is a belief that people can change things without fighting.

**Parliament** (page 46) Parliament is the group of people who make the laws for Great Britain.

**Patriot** (page 55) A Patriot was a person who wanted to be free from Great Britain during the American Revolution.

**pilgrim** (page 28) A pilgrim is a person who makes a trip for religious reasons.

**pioneer** (page 86) A pioneer is a person who goes to live in a new place.

**plantation** (page 40) A plantation is a very large farm.

**plateau** (page 10) A plateau is a high, flat area of land.

**pollution** (page 194) Pollution is dirt or smoke that hurts the air or water.

**Progressives** (page 147) The Progressives were a group of people who worked to make life better in America just before World War I.

**protest** (page 181) To protest is to speak out against something.

**Puritans** (page 30) The Puritans were a group of people who wanted to change the way the English church was run. They wanted to make it more simple, or purer.

**raw materials** (page 100) Raw materials are what factory products, like cloth and tools, are made of.

**recycle** (page 194) To recycle means to use something again.

**regiment** (page 60) A regiment is a team of soldiers.

**repeal** (page 46) To repeal is to take back or do away with something.

**represent** (page 30) To represent means to speak and act for someone.

**reservation** (page 84) A reservation is land the government sets aside for American Indians to live.

**rural** (page 40) A rural area has many farms and few towns or cities.

**satellite** (page 191) A satellite is something that goes around Earth in space.

**secede** (page 110) To secede is to leave.

**segregated** (page 189) Segregated means that one group is kept apart from another group.

**settlement** (page 21) A settlement is a new place where people live. St. Augustine, Florida, was the first settlement in the United States.

**settlement house** (page 132) A settlement house is a place in the neighborhood that helps people.

**settler** (page 41) A settler is a person who goes to live in a new place.

**sharecropper** (page 118) A sharecropper is a person who rents land from a farmer. Sharecroppers pay rent with a share of the crops.

**shares of stock** (page 161) Shares of stock are small parts of businesses that people buy and sell in the stock market.

**slave state** (page 104) Before the Civil War, a slave state was a state that allowed slavery.

**sod** (page 140) Sod is hard soil held together by grass.

**space shuttle** (page 191) A space shuttle is a spaceship that can be used again and again.

**stock market** (page 161) On the stock market people buy and sell shares of stock.

**strike** (page 131) To strike is to refuse to work until changes are made.

**suffrage** (page 158) Suffrage is the right to vote.

**tax** (page 46) A tax is money that people pay for government services.

**tenement** (page 128) A tenement is a building in a poor part of a city.

**tepee** (page 11) A tepee is a tent made of buffalo hides.

**time line** (page 20) A time line is a diagram that shows a period of time.

**totem** (page 10) A totem is something from nature, such as an animal spirit. The Northwest Coast Indians carved totems on tall poles.

**trail drive** (page 141) On a trail drive, cowboys take cattle to the railroad.

**treaty** (page 36) A treaty is a written agreement.

**troops** (page 112) Troops are soldiers.

**uniform** (page 55) A uniform is clothing worn by people in a special group, such as the army.

**victory** (page 54) Victory is the defeat of an enemy.

# Index